W9-BVY-646

Young Readers Edition

EVOLUTION

Ruth Moore

and the Editors of TIME-LIFE BOOKS

TIME-LIFE BOOKS, NEW YORK

ON THE COVER: A chimpanzee displays near-human emotions ranging from curiosity to anger. The naturalist Charles Darwin pointed to such expressions in defense of his theory that man had evolved from early apelike creatures.

LIFE WORLD LIBRARY
LIFE NATURE LIBRRY
TIME READING PROGRAM
THE LIFE HISTORY OF THE UNITED STATES
LIFE SCIENCE LIBRARY
GREAT AGES OF MAN
TIME-LIFE LIBRARY OF ART
TIME-LIFE LIBRARY OF AMERICA
FOODS OF THE WORLD
THIS FABULOUS CENTURY
LIFE LIBRARY OF PHOTOGRAPHY

Published simultaneously in Canada.
Library of Congress catalogue card number 68-8382.
XX

Contents

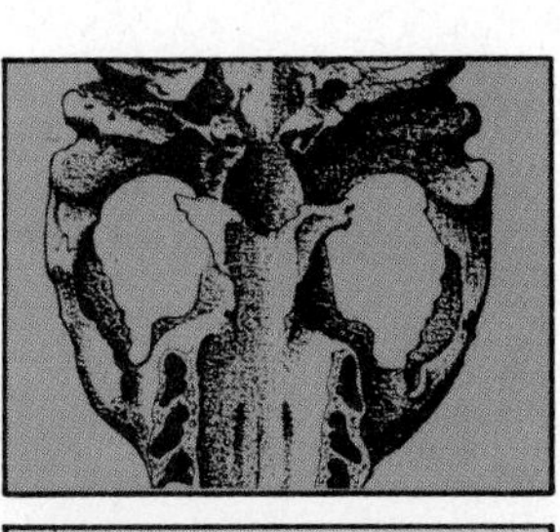

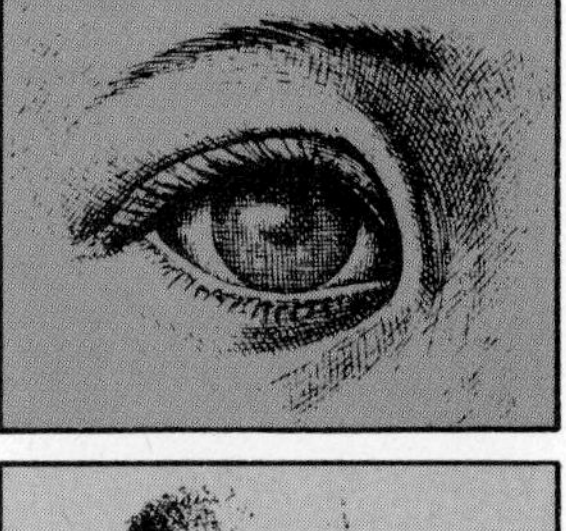

Introduction

Of all the sciences, biology is the most important to an understanding of man. It was slightly more than a century ago, in 1859, that Darwin set forth the revolutionary idea that man, together with every other living thing, is a product of a process of evolutionary development. But human evolution is not all in the past; it is going on now and will concern us deeply in the future. The problem of possible genetic damage from radiation exposures, including those resulting from the fallout from the testing of atomic weapons, has quite properly claimed much popular attention in recent years.

And yet this is only a part, and probably a relatively minor part, of a vastly greater problem: how to maintain the genetic health of the human species. It is becoming more and more evident that man can no longer rely solely on Darwinian natural selection and other "natural" processes to insure his fitness for the environments in which he lives. Here mankind faces possibly the greatest challenge of its whole history as a biological species. The time is not far off when man will have to regulate his numbers, and control the genes he passes on to his descendants so that mankind can remain healthy and vigorous. We must have knowledge and understanding in order to respond successfully to this challenge to survival. To help people gain such knowledge and understanding is the aim of this book.

THEODOSIUS DOBZHANSKY, *Professor*
The Rockefeller University
New York City

1

Darwin's Voyage into the Past

CHARLES DARWIN was 66 years old when this photograph was taken, four years after the publication of his controversial book, *The Descent of Man.* Others had challenged the Bible's version of man's origin, but Darwin put creation firmly on a scientific basis.

A peculiar odor caught the attention of a young English naturalist named Charles Darwin as he walked through a lofty green forest just outside Rio de Janeiro, Brazil. The scent came from a curious, mushroomlike fungus that reminded him of a kind he knew in England, called Phallus. In walks through the woods at home he had often seen beetles alight on the fungus because they had been drawn to the plant by its smell. Now he saw a beetle settle itself on the Brazilian plant, which was called Hymenophallus. Darwin knew that the two plants did not belong to the same family, or species, and the beetles were of different species too. Yet in two countries, far away from each other, the plant and the bug related to each other in the same way. Darwin could not help wondering about this.

The year was 1832 and Darwin was 23, starting a five-year world cruise on H.M.S. *Beagle,* to study plants and animals. He was already finding strange likenesses and differences that the traditional story of creation in the Bible did not explain. According to one famous bishop, every species of plant and animal on earth had come into being at one moment, about 6,000 years ago. But had bee-

A Huge Creature from the Past

The skull of a *Toxodon (right),* a massive animal that once lived in South America, was found by Darwin during the early part of his voyage on the *Beagle.* The discovery supported Darwin's theory that species were not created separately but evolved from common ancestors. Darwin believed that the *Toxodon* was the distant relative of such animals as the elephant and the rhinoceros.

tles been created full-grown, or as larvae? Which had come first, the oak or the acorn, the pumpkin or the seed? And why did many living things bear a resemblance to extinct, fossil creatures?

For years, Darwin tried to find the answers to questions like these. Most people literally believed the traditional story of creation and Darwin did too, at first. Then he began to think that perhaps a single kind of life was the ancestor of all kinds of life on earth today and that these kinds of life became different as they gradually took over the earth, its air and its waters. Darwin did not invent this idea of evolution—one thing changing into another—but he presented more information about it than anyone else had when he wrote two books, long after he had returned to England from his exciting world trip. One book, published in 1859, he titled

On
THE ORIGIN OF SPECIES
by Means of Natural Selection,
or *the Preservation of Favoured Races*
in the Struggle for Life.

The second, published in 1871, he called

THE DESCENT OF MAN
and Selection in Relation to Sex.

Darwin's descriptions of things he saw and of experiments he had made—and his own sensible arguments—gave the whole study of natural science a new kind of foundation that explained life on earth more clearly than the Church had. But the theory of evolution that Darwin wrote about made a great many people angry. It is one thing for man to believe that he was created in the image of God. It is quite another for him to be told that he is merely the product of a billion or so years of ever-evolving life—and that he must trace his beginnings back through mammals and amphibians to the lowly fish, and from there to some unknown, miraculous kind of organism like a molecule.

Charles Robert Darwin was born on February 12, 1809, the same day as Abraham Lincoln. He was the son of Dr. Robert Waring Darwin, a physician, and the grandson of Dr. Erasmus Darwin, who was well-known as a physician, naturalist and poet. Erasmus Darwin's views of nature undoubtedly influenced Charles. "Would it be too bold," he had once written, "to imagine that in the great length of time since the earth began to exist, perhaps millions of ages before the commencement of the history of mankind—would it be too bold to imagine that all warm-blooded animals have arisen from one living filament. . .?"

As Charles Darwin grew up in his father's large house, near Shrewsbury in western England, he often heard his grandfather's ideas discussed. Darwin's mother had died when Charles was eight. Dr. Darwin liked to assemble his children and talk at length on the views of his own father and a wide range of subjects. Young Charles listened with more awe than understanding. He was more interested in collecting pebbles, insects, plants and birds' eggs.

At 16 Charles was absorbed, as his father

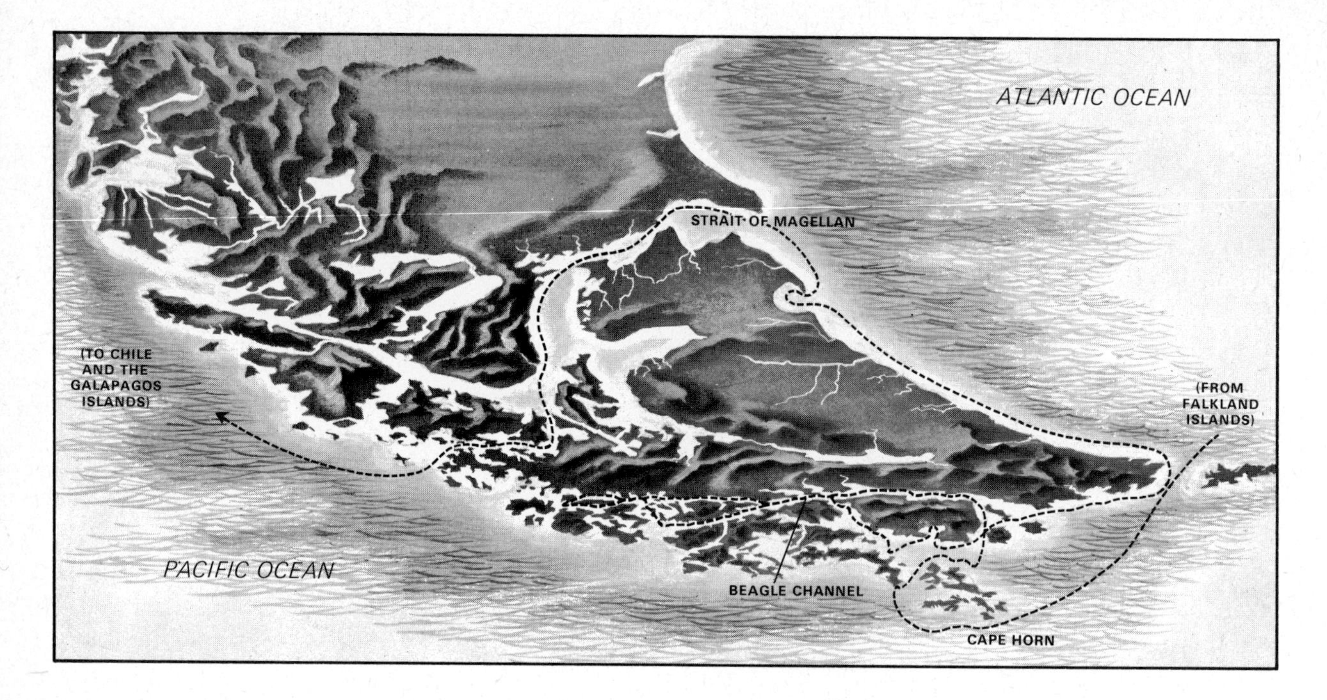

put it, in "shooting, dogs and rat-catching," and was "doing no good" at school. Determined that his son should not grow up into an idle sportsman, Dr. Darwin sent Charles and his older brother Erasmus to the University of Edinburgh to study medicine. There Charles made a required visit to the operating theater. A child was being operated on, and chloroform and ether were not yet in use. Charles ran from the room, never to return.

At about the same time, he learned that he would eventually inherit enough property to live comfortably for all of his life. That ended his studies of medicine. When it became clear that Charles also had no desire to be a lawyer, Dr. Darwin decided that his son should become a clergyman. Always willing to please his father—though seldom able to—Charles agreed. He could accept the creed of the Church of England and he liked the idea of a country church.

From 1828 to 1831 Charles attended Cambridge University, where he did enough work with tutors to get passing grades. The Cambridge he loved, though, was a different one—shooting small game with the sporting crowd, collecting beetles, walking with the Reverend John Stevens Henslow, professor of botany.

He also read the work of a French naturalist, Jean-Baptiste Lamarck, who believed that the simplest living things had given rise to all others and that change had occurred as environment placed a new demand on a particular animal. This demand, Lamarck said, made the animal use its body in new ways; as a result, some parts became larger or longer or stronger than they had been, and others, not used, became smaller or weaker. These changes, he said, were then passed on to the

Men Adapted to Cold

Naked except for a fur cape draped over his knees, an Ona Indian takes aim with bow and arrow while holding his quiver in his mouth. Darwin encountered such Indians when the *Beagle* rounded Cape Horn, the New World's southernmost inhabited land (the ship's route is shown on the map at far left). He saw them canoeing in almost freezing temperatures, wearing little or no clothing. At night they slept naked on the wet, near-frozen ground. Darwin decided that nature had specially fitted these people to their rugged environment.

animal's offspring. As an example, Lamarck liked to refer to the giraffe because its long neck seemed to be such an odd thing for an animal to have. According to the naturalist, the giraffe may have grown from an animal much like an antelope that at some point began to eat the leaves of trees. In order to do this, it had to stretch its neck, tongue and legs. At first these parts of its body were stretched just a little, and the longer neck, tongue and legs were passed on to its offspring. As they grew up, they stretched a little more, and so on, until the present giraffe had developed.

Few people disagreed with Lamarck's theory, mainly because it attracted little attention. Over 50 years later, Charles Darwin would demonstrate that *only* giraffes with long necks had survived to produce more of their kind. And a century would pass before scientists learned that the only characteristics that can be inherited are those "acquired" in the slow, evolutionary way, not those acquired during one lifetime.

At college Darwin also encountered the Greek philosophers' views of creation. Thales, in the Sixth Century B.C., had studied the abundant life of the Aegean Sea and declared water to be "the mother from which all things arose and out of which they exist." Heraclitus, a philosopher, had written that everything is "transposed into new shapes." And Aristotle, another philosopher, had stated that there was a natural progression from plants, to plant-animals, to animals, and then, by graduated steps, to man.

But none of this—the ideas of the Greeks, the thoughts of Erasmus Darwin or the well-worked-out theory of Lamarck—seemed important as the 1830s began. For the Bible declared: "And God said: Let the waters bring forth abundantly the moving creature that hath life. . . . Let the earth bring forth the living creature after his kind. . . . Let us make man in our image. . . ." Furthermore, an Irish expert on the Bible, Archbishop James Ussher, had in the 17th Century translated this to mean that all life had been suddenly and miraculously created in the year 4004 B.C. This date was widely accepted as the true time of creation. Only Noah's Flood, it was argued by scholars, had reshaped life and landscape into the forms known to the 19th Century.

All of this was more than a belief; it was the foundation on which society then stood, the base of man's special status in the universe. Even as Charles Darwin read the quite different views of his grandfather and others, he had no intention of challenging such a fundamental principle. He was not a particularly rebellious young man.

An invitation to join the *Beagle* on an exploratory scientific expedition came soon after Darwin had finished his studies at Cambridge. Charles was excited and eager to go. And Charles' botany teacher, the Reverend Henslow, had written that there "never was a finer chance for a man of zeal and spirit." Dr. Darwin was strongly against the idea; he did not want Charles to change his profession again. But finally he gave in and agreed to finance the trip for his son.

On the 27th of December, 1831, the *Beagle*

A Strange Island World

Darwin spent five weeks exploring the Galápagos Islands, which lie on the equator, west of Ecuador. These islands have bleak, dry lowlands studded with prickly pear cactus trees *(below)*, but their interiors are lush with vegetation. Reptiles and birds thrive there but there are few insects and only two native mammals—a small rat and a bat. Darwin's studies of these isolated species greatly influenced his historic theory of evolution.

THE BEAGLE'S ROUTE THROUGH THE GALÁPAGOS

Darwin's Family of Finches

After studying a group of finches he had collected on the Galápagos Islands, Darwin began to question the popular belief that all animals were created exactly as they are. He had discovered 13 different species of finches on the islands, each displaying differences in size, plumage and

INSECT EATER

WARBLER FINCH

PRIMARILY INSECT EATERS PLUS SOME PLANTS

LARGE INSECTIVOROUS TREE FINCH

MEDIUM INSECTIVOROUS TREE FINCH

SMALL INSECTIVOROUS TREE FINCH

TOOL-USING FINCH

MANGROVE FINCH

sailed from Devonport. The 235-ton brig scarcely had sailed beyond sight of land when Darwin became seasick. As he lay in his hammock he read a new book, Volume I of Charles Lyell's *Principles of Geology*. Lyell was arguing that the earth's continents, plains and mountains were shaped not by Noah's Flood, but by the action of the rains, the winds, earthquakes, volcanoes and other natural forces. To Darwin, reading Lyell as the *Beagle* sailed southward, a new and dazzling array of ideas soon appeared.

On January 16 the *Beagle* came to anchor at Praia in the Cape Verde Islands, off the western bulge of Africa. It was Darwin's first sight of the tropics. Tamarinds, bananas and palm trees—the brilliantly colored scene was "overwhelming and glorious." As he looked eagerly around, he noticed a broad band of white stretching for miles along the face of the sea cliff. Climbing up to investigate, he found embedded in the white stone thousands of sea shells, many of them like the shells he had gathered on the beach below.

With the guidance of Lyell's book, Darwin figured out the reason. The bed of white shells had once been a part of the sea bottom. At some time in the past, a stream of lava had flowed into the sea and covered the bed. The heat of the lava had changed the top layer partly into a crystalline limestone and partly into a compact, spotted stone. Later still, some force inside the earth had raised up the entire coast until the onetime sea bottom stood 45 feet above the water.

As the *Beagle* sailed toward South America on calm and sunny seas, Darwin had a long, bag-shaped net towed behind the ship. He studied and compared the little fish and marine organisms that he hauled in, often in large numbers. Were some of them new or unknown species? If they differed from organisms already known to science, in what respects did they differ?

kinds of beaks. But basically they were alike. Darwin did not believe they could have been created separately and still have so much in common. Thus, he reasoned, evolution working over millions of years had developed the different species from a single common ancestor.

When he reached South America he found the relationships between the animals of the past and those of the present even more striking and upsetting. Along an old river bed in Argentina, Darwin noticed some fossil bones sticking out of the gravel and red mud. He began to dig and unearthed the remains of nine huge, four-legged animals all belonging to species long gone from the earth. One, the *Toxodon,* equaled an elephant in size and yet its teeth were those of a gnawer—an order that in modern times includes mostly the smaller four-footed animals. The position of its eyes, ears and nostrils suggested that it probably had been able to live in the water.

Darwin also dug up a decayed tooth of a horse. The fossil lay in the same layer of earth with teeth of the *Toxodon* and mastodon and the bony armor of a gigantic animal that looked like an armadillo. The presence of the horse's tooth proved that this animal so familiar to us had been among the ancient inhabitants of the continent, even though he had disappeared long before the first Spanish settlers arrived.

The fossil species Darwin was uncovering on the Argentine prairies of South America looked a lot like the known fossil animals of North America. In more recent times each continent had its own kind of animal population—South America its monkeys, llama, tapir, anteater and armadillo, and North America its sheep, ox, goat and antelope. Darwin decided that the later animals were different because they could not travel between the two continents after a land connection sank below the sea.

Darwin also realized that the ancient animals of both continents were closer to the animals of Asia and Europe than were living American species. This probably meant, he decided, that the North American elephants, mastodons, and horses had migrated from Siberia over a land bridge in the area of the

The Seagoing Lizards

The dinosaurlike marine iguana exists only on the Galápagos Islands. Probably because of the swift ocean currents and the shark-infested waters, these iguanas seldom if ever travel between the islands. As a result, different species have evolved on separate islands. The drab iguanas at left are native to Narborough Island, while the colorful iguana at right is found only on Hood Island.

Bering Strait, which separates Alaska from Russia. They gradually made their way to the southern continent, where they finally became extinct.

What actually had happened to the giant four-footed animals whose fossilized bones were scattered across the Argentine plains? Darwin never found out—and neither has anyone else.

Not long after visiting Argentina, the *Beagle* sailed into the stormy waters off Tierra del Fuego at the tip of South America. As the brig dropped anchor in the Bay of Good Success, in December 1832, a band of natives, uttering wild cries, greeted her from the edge of the dense and gloomy forest that extended down to the shore. The next morning Darwin accompanied the *Beagle* party that went ashore to negotiate with them. Broad bands of red and white streaked the face of their leader. Their only clothing consisted of fur skins thrown across the shoulders, "leaving their persons as often exposed as covered," Darwin noted. One woman, nursing a newborn baby, later stood for hours watching the ship while sleet fell and melted on her naked bosom and the naked skin of the child.

Darwin was beginning to understand the great differences between peoples as well as plants and animals. He marveled that a human tribe could live in such a harsh, bleak climate, but the Fuegians did not seem to be dying out. Nature, Darwin concluded, had fitted man to survive even here.

Toward the end of the five-year voyage of the *Beagle,* Darwin crowned all his previous observations with studies of the strange animal life on the Galápagos Islands, about 600 miles off the coast of Ecuador in the Pacific Ocean. The dry, volcanic island chain at first looked bare of any life. But as he walked across the rugged lava surface of one of the

A Lone Survivor of the Past

The tuatara, found only on a few small islands in New Zealand, is a member of a family of "beak-headed" reptiles known as the rhynchocephalians. All of its relatives have been extinct for millions of years. Living in isolation, the tuatara has somehow managed to exist, virtually unchanged.

islands, Darwin suddenly met two huge tortoises—about 200 pounds each—ambling along a well-beaten path. In the strange, empty setting they resembled something that might have lived before Noah built his ark. Darwin later learned that the Galápagos were the tortoises' original home; no other species like them had developed anywhere else in the world.

To Darwin's growing amazement, this unusual situation was repeated. Great black lizards, some four feet long, sunned themselves on the black rocks along the shore. Darwin had read that they often went to sea "in herds a-fishing." The careful naturalist opened the stomachs of several lizards and found minced seaweed. Not only was the black lizard a vegetarian, it was an extraordinary creature: a seagoing lizard. The burrows of another land-living lizard pockmarked the ground on one island so that it was difficult for the *Beagle* party to find a place to pitch a tent. This lizard too was found only in these islands.

The birds of the archipelago were even more remarkable. Darwin shot or captured 26 kinds. All except one far-ranging finch had never been found anywhere else. Among them were 13 finches, "a most singular group of finches," Darwin wrote, for all resembled one another in the structure of their beaks, in the form of their bodies and in their feathers—and yet each was a separate species.

Seeing this variety in finches on one group

(Text continued on page 22)

Krakatoa: Where Life Began Again

One summer morning in 1883 a volcano erupted on the island of Krakatoa near Java. Nothing survived the explosion—not a single animal, plant or seed. But life returned little by little, and as it did, scientists gained some knowledge of how living things originally colonized the earth.

In the key drawing at left, the colors show how various plants and animals arrived—green if by sea, purple if carried by birds, blue if blown by the

wind. The numbers identify different species. First to be seen on the island was a spider (1), found nine months after the eruption. Mosses and ferns (2) and the seeds of flowering plants such as Emilia (3) and Wedelia (4) soon followed, settling on algae that the wind had blown over. The Calophyllum tree (5), the Tournefortia shrub (6) and Ipomoea (7) began to appear, and by 1896 orchids (8) took root. Seeds of tropical trees such as Barringtonia (9), Casuarina (10) and coconut (11) began to grow, and fig trees (12) were soon seen. Except for strong swimmers such as the python (13) and the monitor (14), most reptiles—geckos (15), Calotes (16) and skinks—must have floated to the island, either alive or as eggs, on floating debris. Within 50 years, the island was alive again. A thick young forest had taken root, and over 1,200 species of animals were established.

of islands fascinated Darwin, and he thought that perhaps they had evolved from just one species. He was coming closer to admitting that all things had come from one ancestor.

If only these species had been very different from those in the rest of the world, Darwin's increasing worries about special creation might have stopped. Most of the various species, however, bore a marked resemblance to related groups on the American mainland, some 500 to 600 miles over the sea. If new and different beings had been placed on the islands at the time of creation, why did they bear the American stamp? Such questions ran persistently through Darwin's mind as he prepared to leave the subworld of the Galápagos.

On October 2, 1836, the *Beagle* reached the shores of England. Most of Darwin's collections, as well as his notebooks and carefully kept journal, had been shipped home long since. Now 27 and a seasoned naturalist, Darwin was already seeking a better explanation than "special creation" for the basic unity of the entire living world. But when he hurried off the *Beagle* into the rainy dusk at the port of Falmouth, Darwin was an impatient young man with but one thought—to get back home.

Patriarch of the Galápagos

The giant tortoise, found only on the Galápagos Islands, weighs as much as a quarter of a ton, has a shell as big as a bath tub, and sometimes lives to be more than 100 years old. Darwin, who was fascinated by these huge creatures, clocked them at about 360 yards per hour.

2

A Theory That Shook the World

A BARRED CAGE, the leaf of a Venus's-flytrap captures a struggling katydid, which will become food for this unusual insect-consuming plant. The flytrap attracts its insect food with a sweet-smelling fluid. When an insect brushes against tiny trigger hairs, the trap snaps shut and digests the catch.

Massive fossil bones from the Argentine plains crowded Charles Darwin's lodgings at Cambridge. He had returned to the university to edit his *Beagle* journal for publication and to catalogue all the specimens he had collected on the voyage. As he thoughtfully examined the skull of an ancient fossil anteater, he noted the striking ways in which this horse-sized monster of long ago resembled small, living anteaters of today. The extinct animal bore every mark of being the ancestor of the modern animal. If it was, then every species on earth could *not* have been separately created by "elemental atoms" suddenly flashing into specialized living tissues. Many years later Darwin recalled in his autobiography that this was the moment when he fully faced the revolutionary, disturbing idea of evolution.

As he arranged his Galápagos collections, he noticed again that many living species looked like other living species. Every detail of certain finches indicated that they had developed in their own way from ancestors that had arrived from other islands of the Galápagos group. If each species had been independently created, why should some details have been repeated and others ignored?

The connections between living things and between living and extinct groups fascinated Darwin. He thought about the way breeders of animals select the best males and females. If a breeder wanted a swifter horse, he bred the fastest to the fastest. But how was selection carried on in nature, where there was no breeder to pick and choose? Darwin puzzled over this problem. Then in October 1838 he happened to read Thomas Malthus' already famous "An Essay on the Principle of Population." Malthus argued that the human race would overrun the earth if not held in check by war, famine and disease, and that there was a constant struggle to stay alive. Suddenly Darwin realized that the struggle to live did the same thing that the breeder did when he selected his animals. The better-adapted animals survived and the ill-adjusted ones died. The creatures that remained were the best-fitted for their surroundings. Since the environment changed as time went by, in the long run this would bring about creatures so different that they would be a new species.

I had at last got a theory by which to work," Darwin observed. However, he was so cautious and modest that he did not put it into writing until 1842, when he prepared a 35-page report on the theory. Two years later he enlarged it to a 230-page essay and showed it to a few friends. Later, much later, the things he said here became part of his first book, *The Origin of Species*.

Darwin had married his cousin Emma Wedgwood, and soon after the 1842 report was written they fled "vile, smoky" London where they had lived for a few years. They bought a house called "Down," about 16 miles from town. Darwin's health had become poor, but in the calm routine of country life he wrote several books about things he had discovered on his world trip. All his materials from the trip were now accounted for —except for one barnacle not much bigger than the head of a pin.

Darwin had come upon this tiny sea organism on the coast of Chile, burrowing into a shell instead of clinging, as all proper barnacles did. Before he pressed on with his work on species, he felt that it should be studied. He was such a careful investigator that he spent eight long years of work on barnacles. Although this study was tiresome, it taught Darwin how the simplest kinds of animals can vary in any of their parts.

In 1854, with the last of 10,000-odd tiny barnacles shipped out of the house, Darwin wrote his friend Sir Joseph Dalton Hooker, director of the Kew Botanical Gardens, that he was resuming his work on species. Even so, it was three years before he even began the book he had been planning for so long. By June 1858, 11 chapters were drafted. But Darwin might have buried himself in his vast subject for another 10 years or more if an incredible turn of events had not hustled him into putting it in print. In his mail on June 18 came an essay by Alfred Russel Wallace,

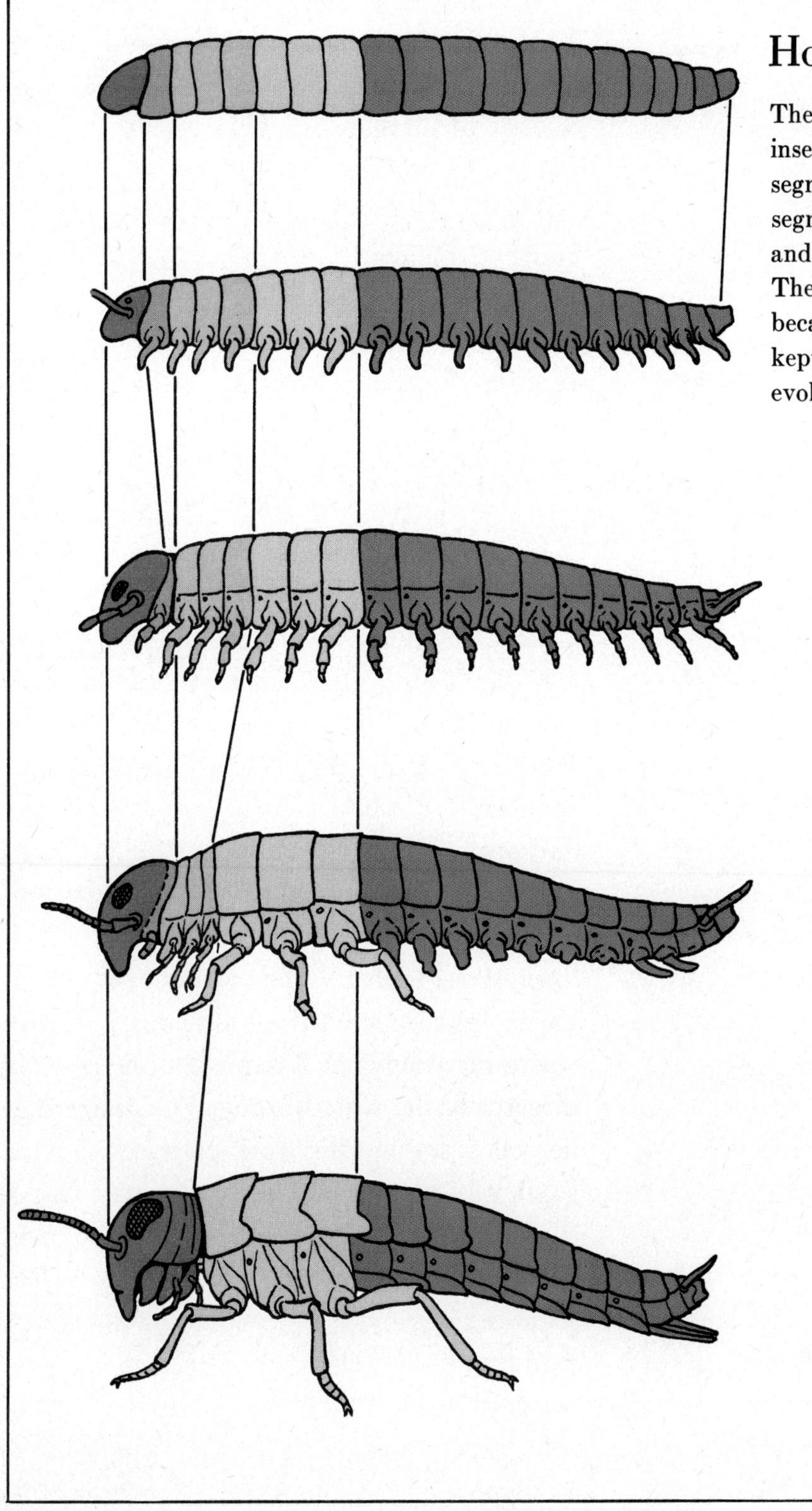

How Insects Evolved

The diagrams at left show how insects could have developed from a segmented worm. The first five segments of the worm grew together and specialized to form the head. The next three sections eventually became the locomotive unit—they kept their legs—and the others evolved into the abdomen.

a naturalist with whom Darwin had been corresponding. In a few pages Wallace had summarized the main points of the theory on which Darwin had spent over two decades.

Stunned, Darwin hurried off a note to the geologist Charles Lyell, who had become a friend: "I never saw a more striking coincidence. . . ." he wrote. "All my originality, whatever it may amount to, will be smashed, though my book, if it will ever have any value, will not be deteriorated, as all the labour consists in the application of the theory." He said he would of course offer Wallace's work for publication, although Wallace had asked him only to forward it, if he thought it good enough, to Lyell. Darwin wondered though if he could honorably publish his own work now. "I would far rather burn my whole book than that he or any other man should think I had behaved in a paltry spirit."

Both Lyell and Hooker, who was also informed of the crisis, acted fast. They suggested that Wallace's paper and Darwin's 1844 essay both be read to a group of scientists who belonged to the Linnean Society.

The Linnean members listened in shocked silence to the novel ideas. Nevertheless, Darwin began to prepare his book for early publication, entitled *The Origin of Species.* It was published November 24, 1859. The first edition's 1,250 copies were all sold the first day, and the storm of rage from the first readers, one that has never wholly died down, quickly broke. The *Quarterly Review* charged that the book and its theory "contradict the revealed relation of the creation to the Creator." One publication accused Darwin of using "absurd facts to prop up his utterly rotten fabric of guesswork and speculation." Darwin had tried not to stir up arguments, and had decided not to discuss the origin of man in *The Origin of Species.* However, he added one meaningful sentence to his last chapter: "Much light will be thrown on the origin of man and his history."

That sentence, along with the ideas in the book, caused a leading scientific magazine to damn Darwin for believing "that man descends from the monkeys." Even Charles Lyell was not sure about man's origin. At a meeting of the British Association for the Advancement of Science at Oxford in June 1860, the outrage still was growing. Word spread that Samuel Wilberforce, the Bishop of Oxford, would take the platform to "smash Darwin," who was not present. When the bishop appeared, a crowd of 700 filled every inch of the meeting room. For half an hour the bishop criticized Darwin fiercely and then, turning to Thomas H. Huxley, a defender of Darwin, he asked a sneering question: Was it through his grandfather or his grandmother that Huxley claimed descent from an ape?

"The Lord hath delivered him into mine hands!" Huxley excitedly whispered to his neighbor on the platform, and strode forth to answer. He told the audience that he would feel no shame at having an ape for an ancestor—but that he would indeed be ashamed of a brilliant man who discussed

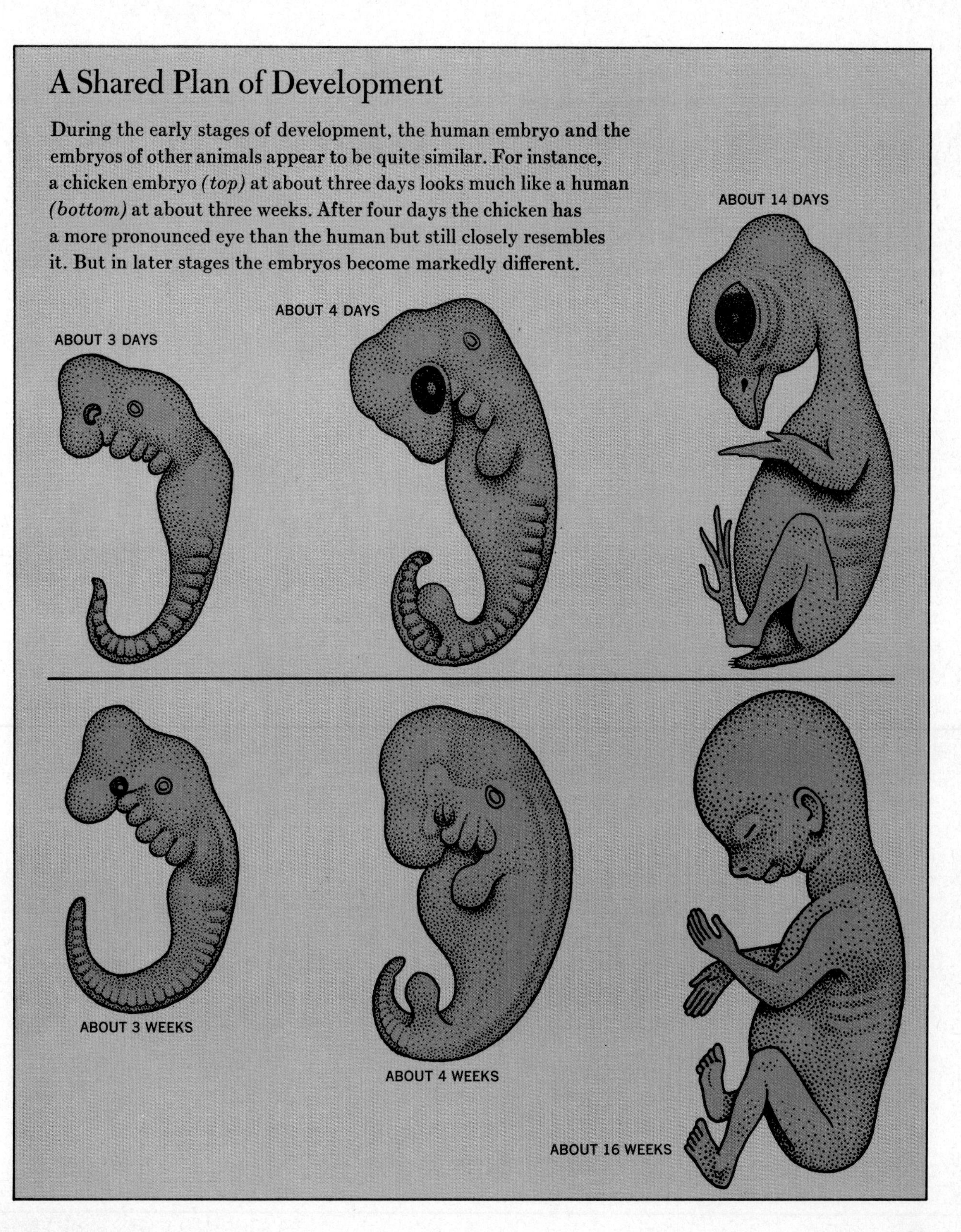
A Shared Plan of Development
During the early stages of development, the human embryo and the embryos of other animals appear to be quite similar. For instance, a chicken embryo *(top)* at about three days looks much like a human *(bottom)* at about three weeks. After four days the chicken has a more pronounced eye than the human but still closely resembles it. But in later stages the embryos become markedly different.
ABOUT 3 DAYS
ABOUT 4 DAYS
ABOUT 14 DAYS
ABOUT 3 WEEKS
ABOUT 4 WEEKS
ABOUT 16 WEEKS

"PROMINENT" MOTH

BLACK AND WHITE NOCTUID MOTH

scientific questions he knew nothing about. In other words, Huxley was saying, he would prefer an ape to the bishop for an ancestor. The crowd knew what he meant.

Darwin's arguments in his book were based on three major facts. First, all living things vary. Second, ". . . we may confidently assert that all plants and animals are tending to increase . . . and that this tendency to increase must be checked by destruction at some period of life." Third, despite the tendency of groups to increase, the numbers of a particular kind of bird or a rabbit, or any species, actually tend to remain almost the same year in and year out. From these facts Darwin decided that there is a struggle for existence among living things, and that only the fittest survive.

Few people could dispute that all living things vary. Each person must know that he is different from all others—unless he is an identical twin. Why each individual should be born different, Darwin could not say. He was acutely aware, however, that the birth of billions of varying individuals had not produced impossible confusion. On the contrary, the living universe was divided into groups and subgroups, and all the individuals seemed to fit together and to suit the conditions of their lives.

The second fact was also clear to see. Darwin believed that every living being tends to increase at so fast a rate that the offspring of a single pair, if not destroyed, would eventually cover the earth. In Darwin's own day even man, a relatively slow breeder, had doubled in number; he calculated that if people increased at such a rate for a thousand years, not even standing room would be left on our

WHITE SPOTTED MOTH

OWLET MOTH

planet. Yet no one species had taken over the world. Darwin came to the conclusion that as living things multiplied, all had to struggle in order to survive.

By a struggle for survival, Darwin did not mean simply a battle of tooth and claw. He included the way one being depends for its preservation on its relations with other beings and its surroundings, and upon its success in creating offspring. In this sense, a plant on the edge of the desert could be said to fight for life because there was no rain, or a mistletoe could struggle with other fruit-bearing plants to tempt birds to eat it and thus to scatter its seeds so it could multiply.

One homely experiment helped Darwin to understand how intense this struggle for life really was. On the lawn outside his living-room window, he marked out a three-by-four-foot plot and let the weeds grow in it.

The Moths' Disappearing Act

The four night-flying moths pictured here spend most of their days in safe concealment simply by hanging flat against tree trunks. They so resemble certain types of bark that they become almost invisible to their enemies. The "prominent" moth at far left, for example, seems to disappear when placed against pine bark, while the black and white noctuid moth, easily spotted when flying, virtually vanishes against birch bark. In the same way, the white spotted moth blends perfectly with the lichens that cover many trees, and the drab owlet moth matches many dark, rough barks.

A Moth Suited to Soot

The English peppered moth in its countryside surroundings was perfectly camouflaged to match the light-colored, spotted lichens on tree trunks, where it rested during the day. But from time to time a mutation occured—a peppered moth that was jet black. As seen in the drawing at top right, this black moth did not have the benefit of camouflage and was quickly spotted and eaten by birds. But when factories began to spew soot across the countryside, many tree trunks were covered with soot. Suddenly the pale moth was easy to see while the black mutant had the advantage of camouflage *(bottom)*. Today the pale moths have been nearly wiped out in industrial areas, but the black mutants thrive.

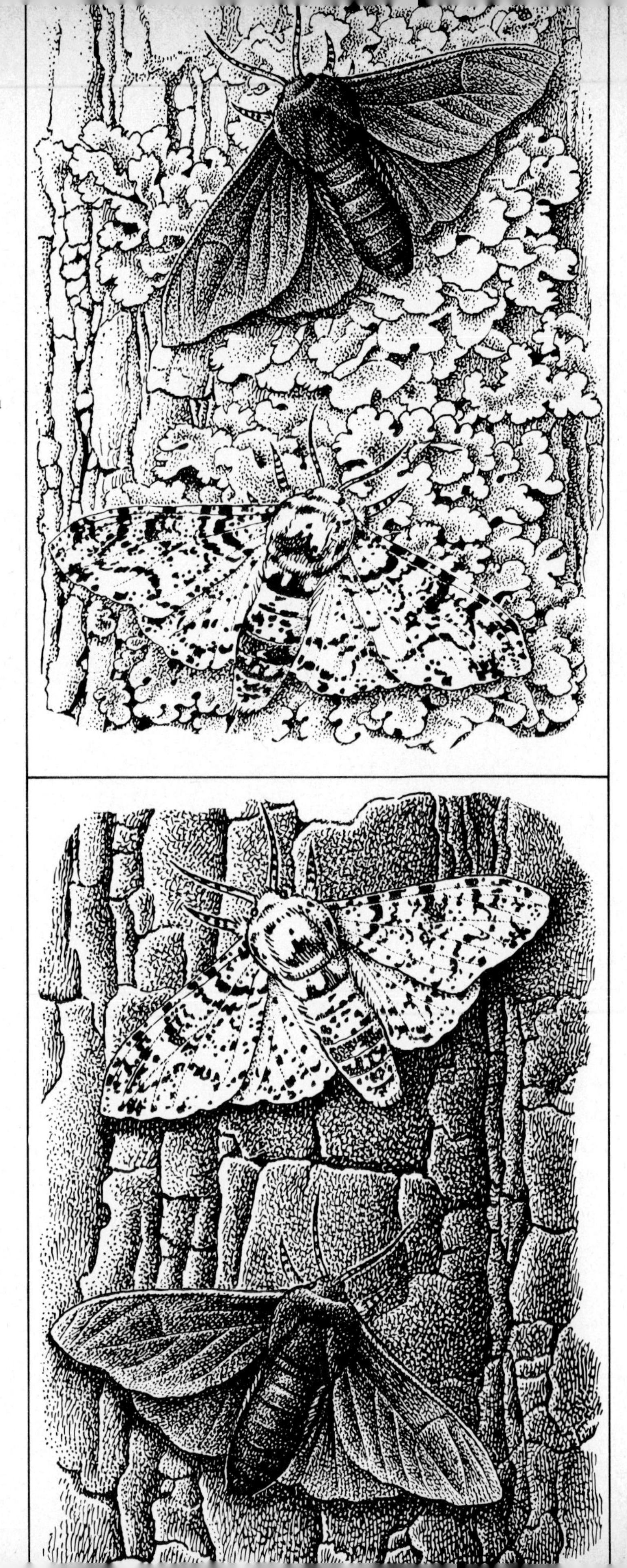

He knew that the stronger plants would kill off the others, but he did not know how many were strong enough to live. During the experiment, he counted 20 different species growing in his little plot. In time, he found that 11 of these survived and nine died.

In thinking about survival, Darwin made his second all-important deduction, which he referred to as "natural selection." He knew that if all members of a group were born alike, survival would be a matter of luck. But he also knew that all members of a species are not alike. Some are stronger, some swifter; some are more or less easily seen. For example, among white grouse, the white feathers of some birds match the white of the snow better than the feathers of other birds. The grouse with a good match can hide better from its enemies, and thus has a better chance to survive and time to give birth to young birds that also are likely to have this protective coloring. This passing on of a difference, or variation, that is helpful in the fight to survive is what Darwin meant by the term natural selection.

But could a lot of small variations add up to bigger differences that would make a whole new species? The question went to the heart of Darwin's case. Common knowledge and his own careful data showed that by adding a number of slight variations, men had been able to produce horses as different as the sleek Arabian and the sturdy Percheron. The two breeds had become so different it was difficult to realize that both had sprung from a common ancestor. How could this have happened naturally, without man's interference?

One day as Darwin was out riding in his carriage, the answer came to him. As the offspring of a species became more and more different from each other they could live in places that varied a great deal. Mammals equipped to fly or swim or climb found new opportunities. The different survived and multiplied; less improved groups died out.

Yet, if life had sprung from one beginning and had occupied the earth by becoming different and moving into other dwellings, proof had to be supplied that it could have reached some of the most faraway parts of the world, such as the distant Galápagos Islands. If a single place on the earth contained life which could not have got there naturally, Darwin's whole case for evolution faced collapse.

Darwin thought that seeds might have floated to the islands. Hooker, the expert botanist, said that seeds would never grow after being in salt water for long. Darwin decided to test this. He placed seeds in bottles of salt water and dropped them in a tank of water cooled to 32°. After a week the seeds had put forth so much mucus that Darwin jokingly said he half expected them to turn into tadpoles. But when he planted them, they grew. In later experiments some seeds survived 137 days' soaking in salt water. Since the ocean current between Ecuador and the Galápagos Islands moves from 13 to 27 miles a day, seeds could easily survive the trip from the mainland about 600 miles away.

Perhaps there were other means of transport too. Seeds might also float to distant islands on driftwood or be carried on the mud-caked feet of birds. It was harder to see how fresh-water shells could have bridged long stretches of salt water to reach fresh water on the islands. Darwin complained that the problem was driving him wild. He was not able to solve the problem until one day when he noticed that ducks coming out of a pond had duckweed caught on their feet. Darwin saw his answer, for he knew that shells live on the weeds. He dangled the feet of a duck in an aquarium where fresh-water shells were just hatching. Immediately a number of shells climbed aboard. They survived out of water for from 12 to 20 hours, time enough for a duck to fly 600 or 700 miles and alight on a fresh-water lake on some far island. Darwin had explained how both the seeds and shells traveled.

Since Darwin's time, scientists have uncovered ancient fossils in all parts of the world. Some are amazingly alike. These discoveries suggest that hundreds of millions of years ago our continents and islands were enormously large land masses—or perhaps a single, huge land mass. As the land became divided, the organic beings became separated. This theory offers another explanation for organic life being in places that are now isolated by large bodies of salt water.

Along with all his experiments, Darwin kept thinking that man came under the same laws as all other living things. Because of his book, this idea was now being discussed free-

A World of Clever Disguises

Some insects, like the bumblebee moth shown sharing a flower with a bee at right, impersonate dangerous animals to protect themselves. The moth matches the bee's form and color, but lacks its stinger. Others, like the Caligo butterfly *(lower right)*, startle foes with deceptive markings. This butterfly's pattern resembles the head of an owl *(below)*—an enemy of the butterfly's enemies.

Nature's Armored Animals

The pangolin *(above)* and the porcupine *(left)* are mild-tempered creatures who, without their specialized coats to defend them, might have been killed off long ago by predators. They rely on their armor for protection, for neither will ever attack. However, both will fight when provoked. The pangolin, whose home is Africa and southern Asia, can give an enemy a vicious swat with its heavy tail. So can the porcupine, leaving its persecutor bristling with pointed, barbed and painful quills.

ly. Darwin hoped that Lyell or some other scientist would write a book examining the problem of man's ancestry and position, but no one did. In time Darwin decided to deal with the subject himself. In February 1867, he began a book that became *The Descent of Man, and Selection in Relation to Sex.*

If man is descended from "some pre-existing form," Darwin wrote, four questions would have to be answered "yes." They were: Does man vary like the other animals? Does he increase so rapidly that there is a struggle for existence in which the most helpful variations are preserved and the least favorable eliminated? Does his body show traces of his descent? Could his high, special qualities of mind and character have appeared as he slowly changed into his present form?

In *The Origin* Darwin had already answered the first two questions. Now he worked for four years on the other two. In his view it was "notorious that man is constructed on the same general type or model as other mammals." This went for all the bones in his body, the structure of his brain, his reproductive processes, even his tendency to infection. Even stranger, man bore within him things that were useless to his modern way of life but had been useful in his past. There were his wisdom teeth, once used for heavy chewing, his appendix, which once had stored food, and his coccyx, the remnant of a tail.

To Darwin, all this evidence was proof of man's descent from another form. Then what about man's mental powers and moral sense? Darwin set out to show that while the gulf between man and the highest apes is immense, the difference is in degree. Animals clearly feel pleasure and pain; in terror their muscles trembled and their hearts thumped like man's. Maternal love, self-sacrifice, jealousy and love of praise, imitation, attention, memory—these qualities and powers did not belong only to man.

As best he could, Darwin tested his arguments. Curious about the curiosity of monkeys, he carried a stuffed snake into the monkey cage at the Zoological Gardens. After the first wild excitement quieted, the monkeys gathered around and stared at it. Then Darwin brought in a paper bag containing a live snake; one by one, the monkeys sidled up to peer into the bag for a peak at the dreadful

A Living Rock Garden

Native to South Africa, the plants shown above and at right are called "stone plants" or "living stones," for they not only grow in stonelike shapes but also take on the color of stones. So successfully have they evolved to match their surroundings that they frequently elude even the keenest collector's eye. Their disguise has served them well, for in South Africa's dry, rock-strewn landscapes they would have been devoured by hungry, thirsty browsing animals if they appeared to be edible.

The Efficient Honeybee

Dusted with pollen, a bee *(left)* gathers nectar from a goldenrod blossom. Dependent on nectar and pollen for nourishment, the honeybee has evolved a remarkable set of tools to help it gather and store its food more efficiently. Three of these tools are indicated in white in the drawing of a honeybee at right. On the bee's rear legs are pollen baskets used to carry pollen to the hive. At the joint of its middle legs is a sharp spur to remove wax from glands on the abdomen—the wax is used to build cells in the honeycomb. And each front leg has a special joint with a comb for cleaning the eyes, and a notch through which antennae are drawn to remove tiny bits of pollen.

object. Darwin also answered the argument that language is a total barrier between beast and men: he showed, with his own pets, that dogs can understand words and sentences, and he pointed out that many birds, besides parrots, can "speak."

The vast gap between the social instincts of an animal and the highest qualities of human beings did not seem to be much greater to Darwin than the distance between the mind of an idiot and that of a genius, or between the most crude human society and the most civilized one. In Darwin's time, some respected scientists believed that man came into the world a civilized being. Savages, they said, had deteriorated from this state.

Darwin believed he had a truer and more cheerful view. He thought that man had risen, by slow and interrupted steps, from "some primordial cell" through the fish, the amphibians and the mammals to an early, apelike creature. From that point on, he held, the development of upright posture and a larger brain could bring enough modification to produce modern man. But Darwin constantly had to face the taunt: "Where are the missing links? Why has none of them been found?" In *The Descent* he could only say that the discovery of fossils is a slow and chancy process at best, and that the regions most likely to hold remains that connected man with his extinct ancestors had not been searched. He admitted with sorrow that the long pedigree he was giving man was not of "noble quality." But he saw no reason to be ashamed of it: "The most humble organism is something much higher than the inorganic dust under our feet; and no one with an unbiased mind can study any living creature, however humble, without being struck with enthusiasm at its marvelous structure and properties."

As he worked on his argument for the descent of life and man, he was troubled by a major difficulty. All animals of a species had to deal with the same conditions and the same struggle, and yet there were differences between the sexes, such as the greater size, strength and fierceness of the male, its weapons of offense or means of defense, its gaudy coloring and ornaments, its power of song.

Darwin decided that besides natural selection which affects both sexes, there must be a kind of sexual selection. "It seems to me almost certain that if the individuals of one sex were during a long series of generations to prefer pairing with certain individuals of the other sex . . . the offspring would slowly but surely become modified in the same manner," he wrote. In 13 lengthy chapters Darwin examined the results of sexual selection in all the large classes of the animal kingdom —the mammals, birds, fish, reptiles and crustaceans. These chapters were really a second book. On February 24, 1871, *The Descent of Man* was published. "On every side it is raising a storm of mingled wrath, wonder, and admiration," said the *Edinburgh Review*. Charles Darwin had gone far in accounting for the likeness and differences of the living world. All life is one, he had shown, because all life has arisen from one unremembered beginning. A new prospect opened, one that was full of progress and of tumult.

The Importance of Being Attractive

The peacock's large and dazzling tail helps this colorful bird to survive. Darwin found that "beauty is sometimes even more important than success in battle," and that the male who can best attract the female will best ensure large numbers of offspring and the continuation of its kind.

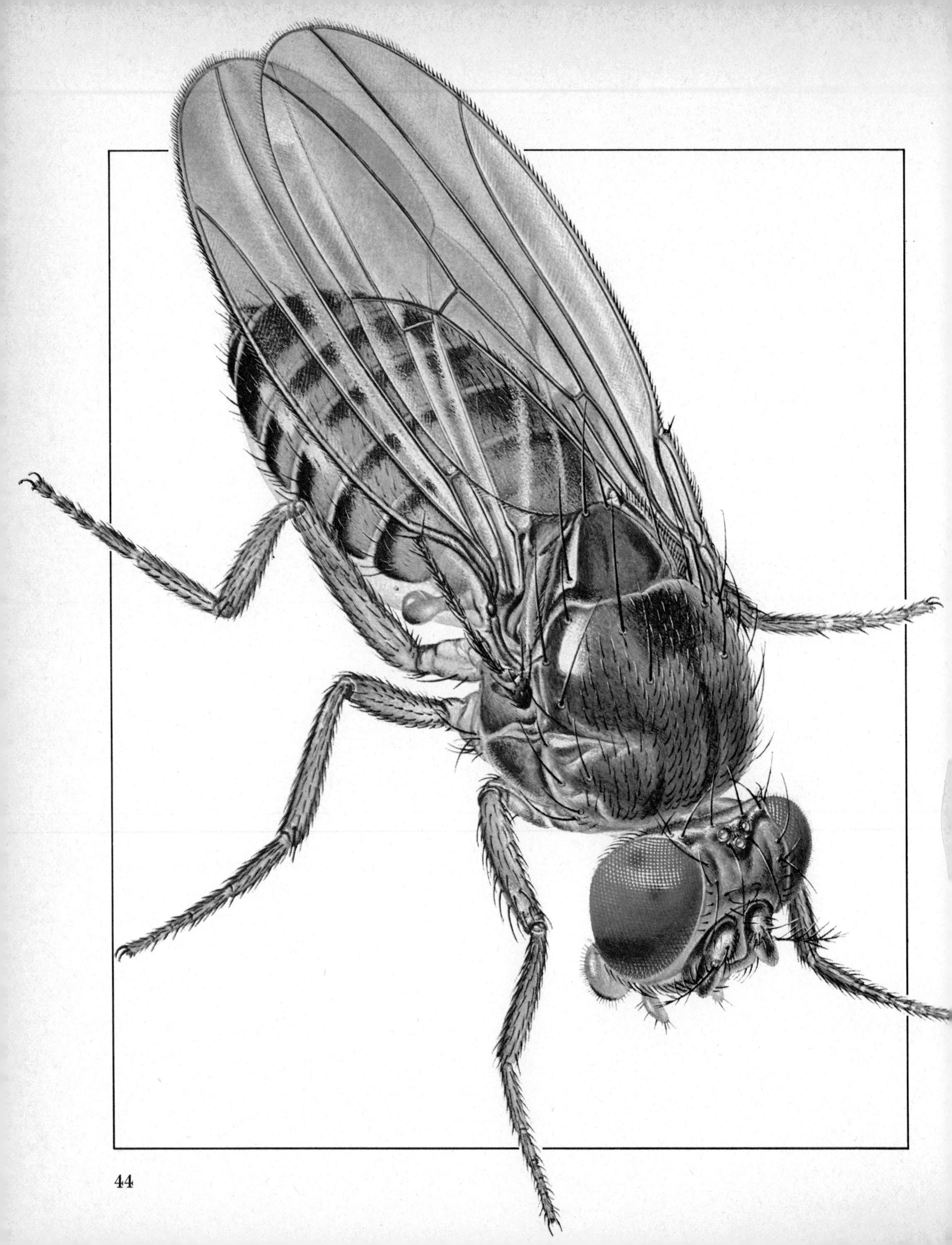

3

Solving the Riddle of Heredity

THE COMMON FRUIT FLY, called *Drosophila melanogaster,* has been man's "guinea pig" in studying animal heredity. The tiny insect produces great numbers of offspring every 10 to 15 days, and millions are used every year to learn more about the hereditary units called chromosomes.

For decades after Darwin wrote about evolution, the big question remained: why are living things different and how do the differences occur? No one could say. To complicate the problem, there seemed to be no reliable rules that controlled what was handed down from parent to offspring. Often a child with black-haired parents would show up with red hair inherited from a grandparent or an even more remote ancestor. Baffled, people believed that such qualities were somehow passed on with the blood, and that a child bore a blend of the "bloods" of his parents. So deeply was the idea rooted that it became a part of the language—as in the expression "a prince of the royal blood."

Darwin was troubled for years by this problem. In an attempt to discover how traits are inherited, he experimented with the garden pea and other plants. For all the carefulness of his work, he could never figure out a pattern of inheritance. Nor, apparently, could anyone else.

In 1856, however, an Austrian monk named Gregor Johann Mendel launched a series of experiments that would show how inheritance, like evolution, is not a matter of

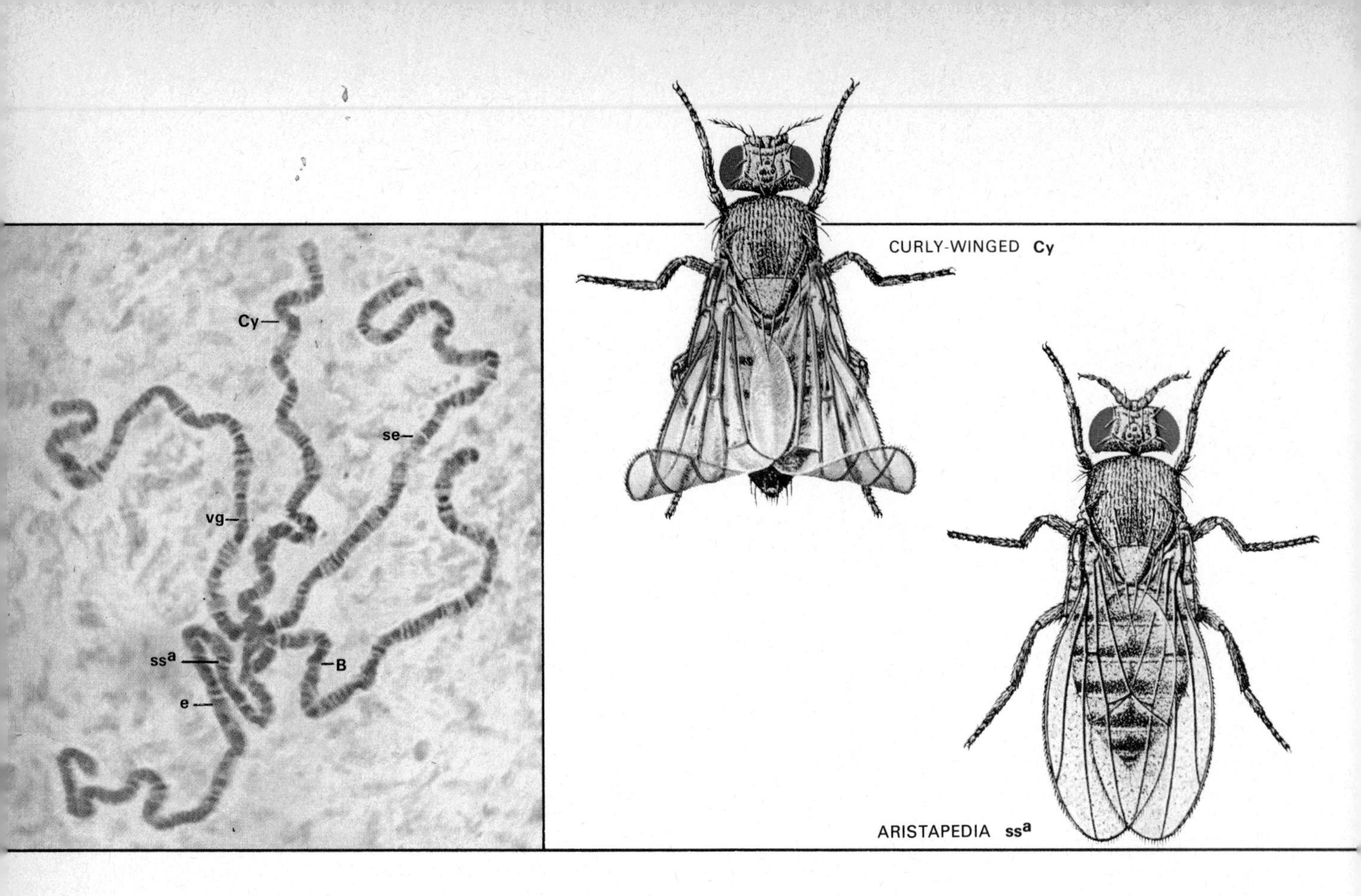

chance or miracle but a matter of law.

Mendel was born on July 22, 1822, in the little village of Heinzendorf. His father, Anton, was known for his fine fruit trees, and he taught young Johann how to improve them with grafts from the orchards of the local manor house.

The Mendels were proud that Johann did so well in his classes, and that he was recommended for higher schooling. There was little money to pay his expenses, but the earnest youngster was sent to a good school some distance away. Sometimes Johann's mother sent baskets of food to him. Even so, he was often hungry and tired. By the time he was 20, he knew that he had better look for a profession in which he would not have to worry constantly about food, shelter and clothing. A teacher suggested that he enter the Augustinian monastery at Brünn. When he was accepted in 1843, Mendel gratefully started his studies there. As an apprentice monk, he took the name of Gregor.

From his youth Mendel, as he once said, had been "addicted to the study of Nature." In the monastery he had time to work on botanical experiments, and he began to breed certain kinds of flowers with others. He soon discovered that when he crossed certain varieties the same characteristics kept appearing again and again. To find out what was happening he also began some experiments with white and gray mice. The books he consulted helped very little. Many studies of hybridization, or the crossing of two varieties, had been made, but the individuals that resulted from hybridization followed no rule.

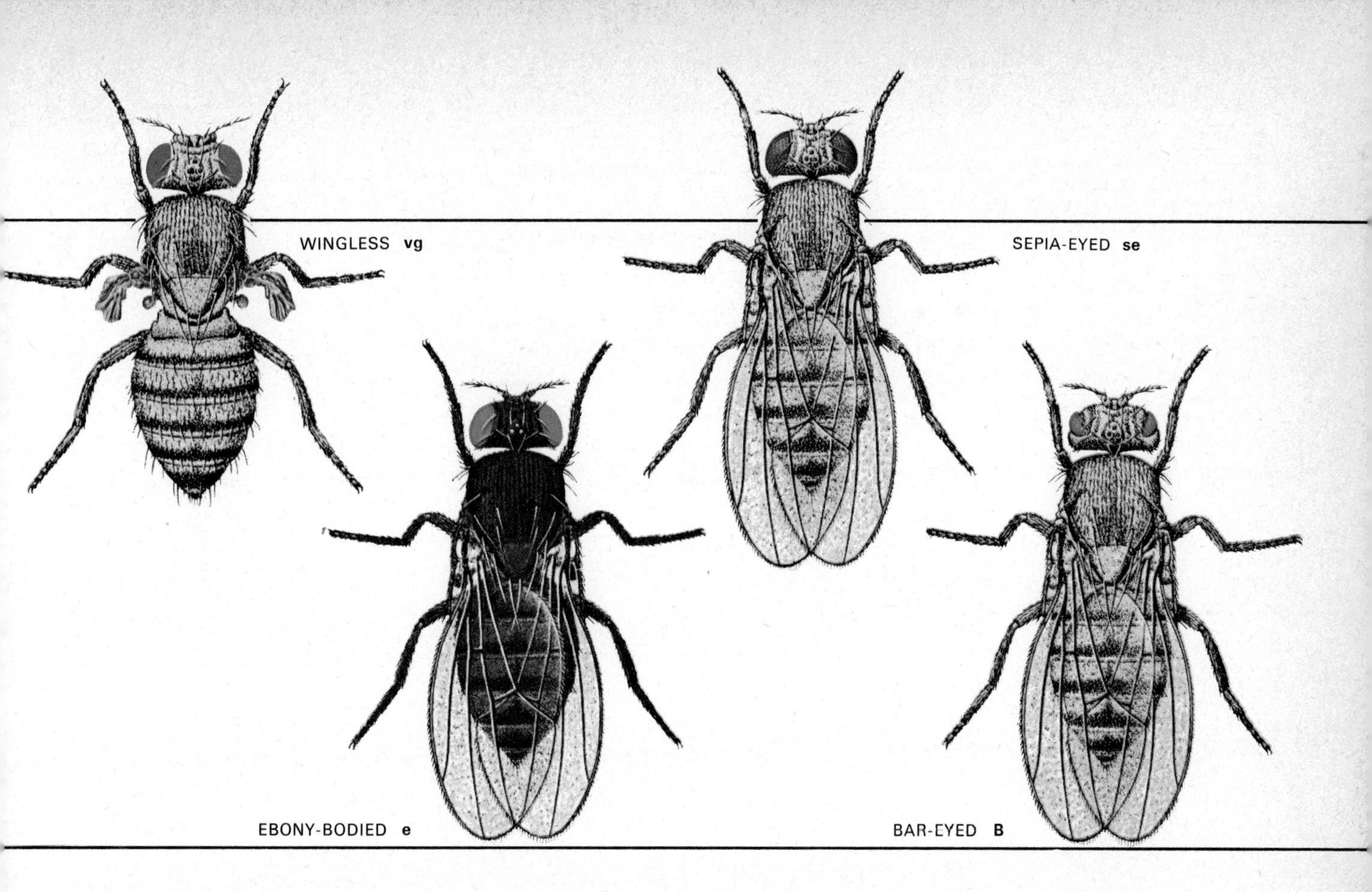

They occurred in all sizes, colors and forms.

It seemed to Mendel that the studies themselves had been carelessly done. No one had bred hybrids for generation after generation and recorded *exactly* what characteristics appeared in each plant. In fact, no one had worked out the kinds of experiments that would make this possible. Mendel decided to take on this task himself.

To begin with, he needed a true breeding plant, one that would always have the same kind of flower as its parent plants. He also needed a plant easily protected from all foreign pollen, which could ruin an experiment. After some testing Mendel chose the common garden pea, because the pea ordinarily fertilizes itself and is easily protected from outside pollen.

Once he had selected the varieties of seeds

Variations Controlled by Genes

The threadlike shapes shown in the picture at the far left are the greatly magnified chromosomes of a fruit fly. Chromosomes occur in all living things and are composed of genes—bits of chemical matter that control all aspects of life. The genes damaged at the points marked by letters have produced the odd flies shown above (in Aristapedia, the antennae have become leglike). Scientists have created many such mutant strains by bombarding the parents' genes with X-rays.

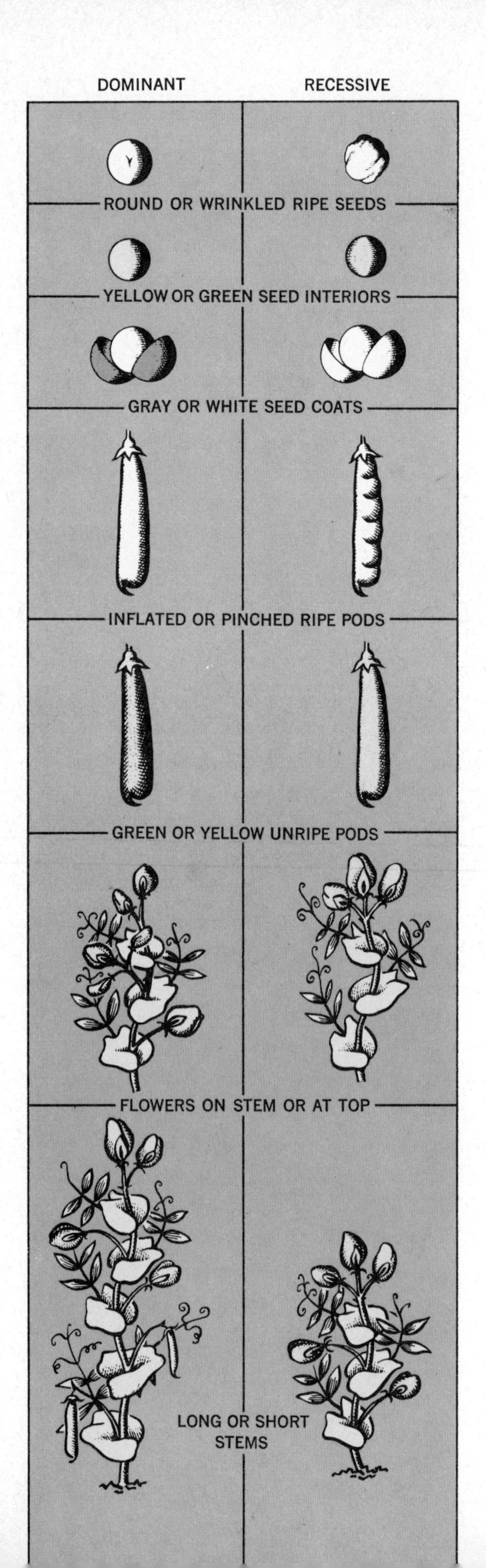

Scientific Truths from Peas

An Austrian monk named Gregor Johann Mendel *(above)* founded the scientific study of heredity over 100 years ago. To find out why the offspring of plants or animals were sometimes like their parents and sometimes unlike them, he bred different varieties of peas and observed how seven obvious pairs of characteristics *(left)* were transmitted from generation to generation. A characteristic that offspring usually inherited from either parent, such as round seeds, he called "dominant"; its opposite was labeled "recessive."

for this experiment, he decided to base his studies on seven comparisons. They were:

(1) The form of the ripe seeds—round or wrinkled.

(2) The color of the peas—yellow or bright green.

(3) The color of the seed coats—gray or white.

(4) The form of the ripe pods—inflated or pinched between the seeds.

(5) The color of the unripe pods—green or vivid yellow.

(6) The positions of the flowers—distributed along the stem or bunched at the top.

(7) The length of the stem—long (six or seven feet) or short (9 to 18 inches).

Mendel was now ready to produce hybrids. He decided to start by crossing wrinkled seeds with round seeds. As soon as the buds formed on the vines, Mendel opened those of each "wrinkled" plant and pinched off the stamens, the part of the blossom that makes pollen for fertilization. To keep any chance pollen from being carried in, he tied a little paper bag around each bud. Then he collected pollen from the round-seed plants, removed the protective bags from the wrinkled-pea buds, and dusted the pollen onto the stigmas, from which pollen is carried deep into the flower to fertilize its seeds. Altogether he made 287 fertilizations on 70 plants.

Then he could only wait until time, sun and rain performed their work. Finally he was able to open the pods of his round-wrinkled hybrids. In them nestled only round peas. The wrinkling, a trait of half of the

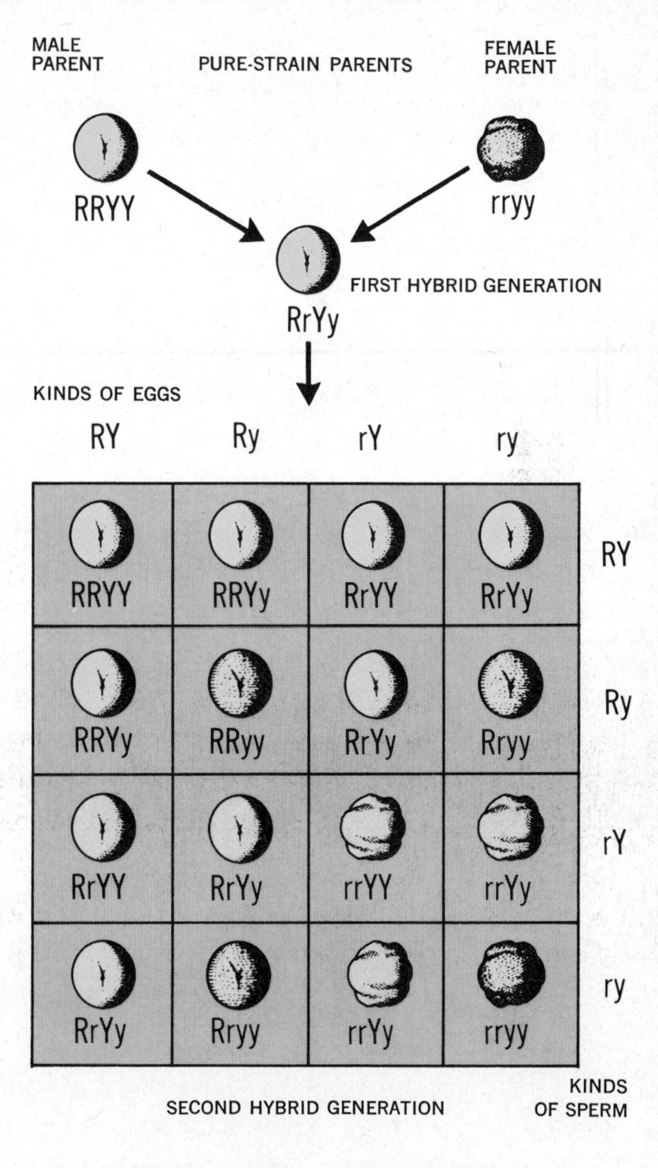

Two Generations of Hybrids

The diagram above shows how pea plants produce different kinds of offspring. A male parent plant *(top)* with only dominant round and yellow traits (RRYY) and a female parent with only recessive wrinkled and green ones (rryy) produce offspring *(center)* that have mixed genes (RrYy) yet look like the male because its genes dominate. When the offspring are interbred *(square)*, they produce four types of peas, of which nine will be round and yellow, three round and green, three wrinkled and yellow, and one wrinkled and green.

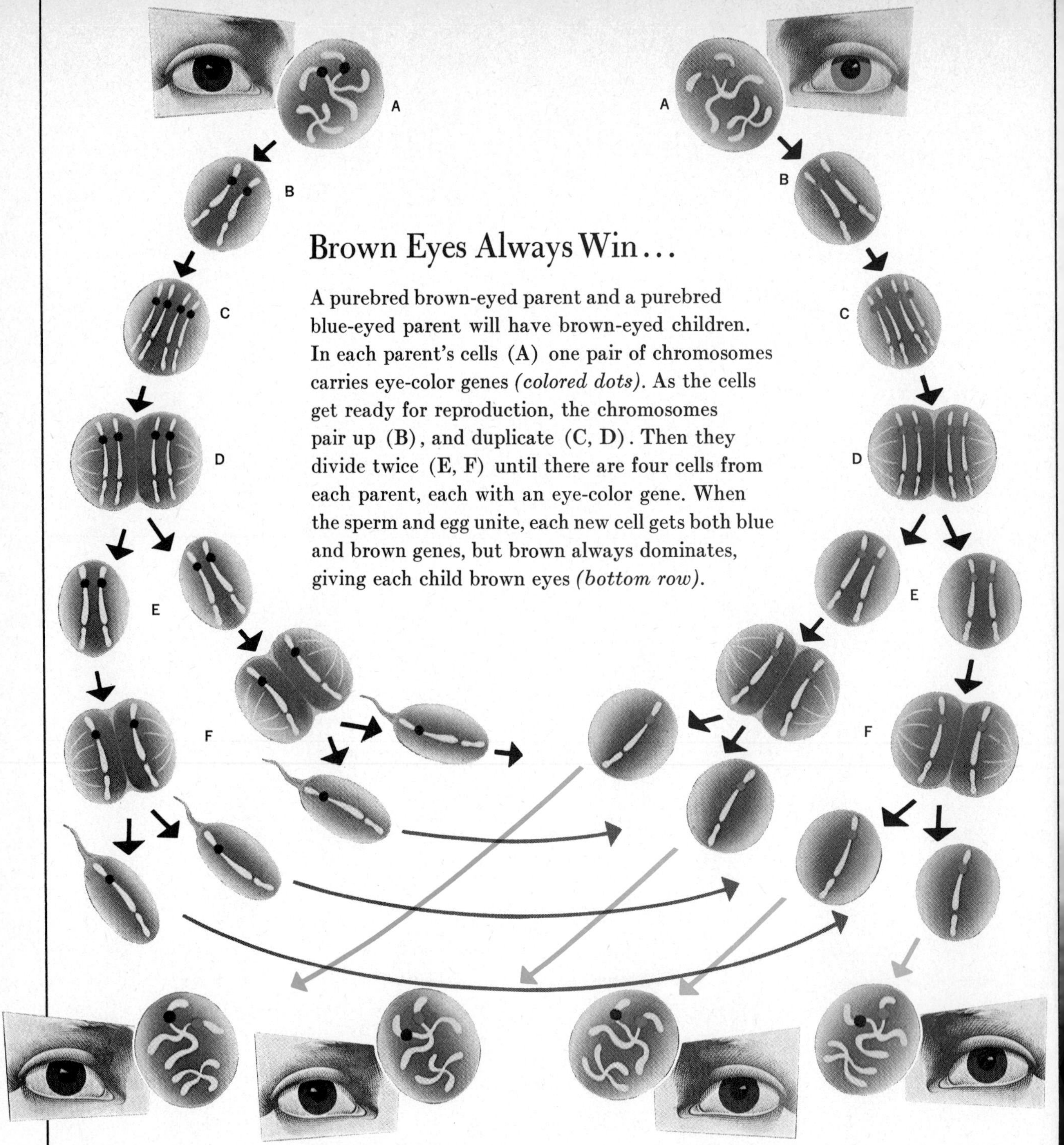

Brown Eyes Always Win...

A purebred brown-eyed parent and a purebred blue-eyed parent will have brown-eyed children. In each parent's cells (A) one pair of chromosomes carries eye-color genes *(colored dots)*. As the cells get ready for reproduction, the chromosomes pair up (B), and duplicate (C, D). Then they divide twice (E, F) until there are four cells from each parent, each with an eye-color gene. When the sperm and egg unite, each new cell gets both blue and brown genes, but brown always dominates, giving each child brown eyes *(bottom row)*.

parent plants, had disappeared completely. So it was with the other six characteristics of his test plants.

As Mendel worked with his jars of labeled pea seeds, he decided to call the characteristic that prevailed (like roundness or yellowness) a "dominant," and the one that disappeared (like wrinkledness or greenness) a "recessive." Thanks to his methodical approach, he knew what had gone into his

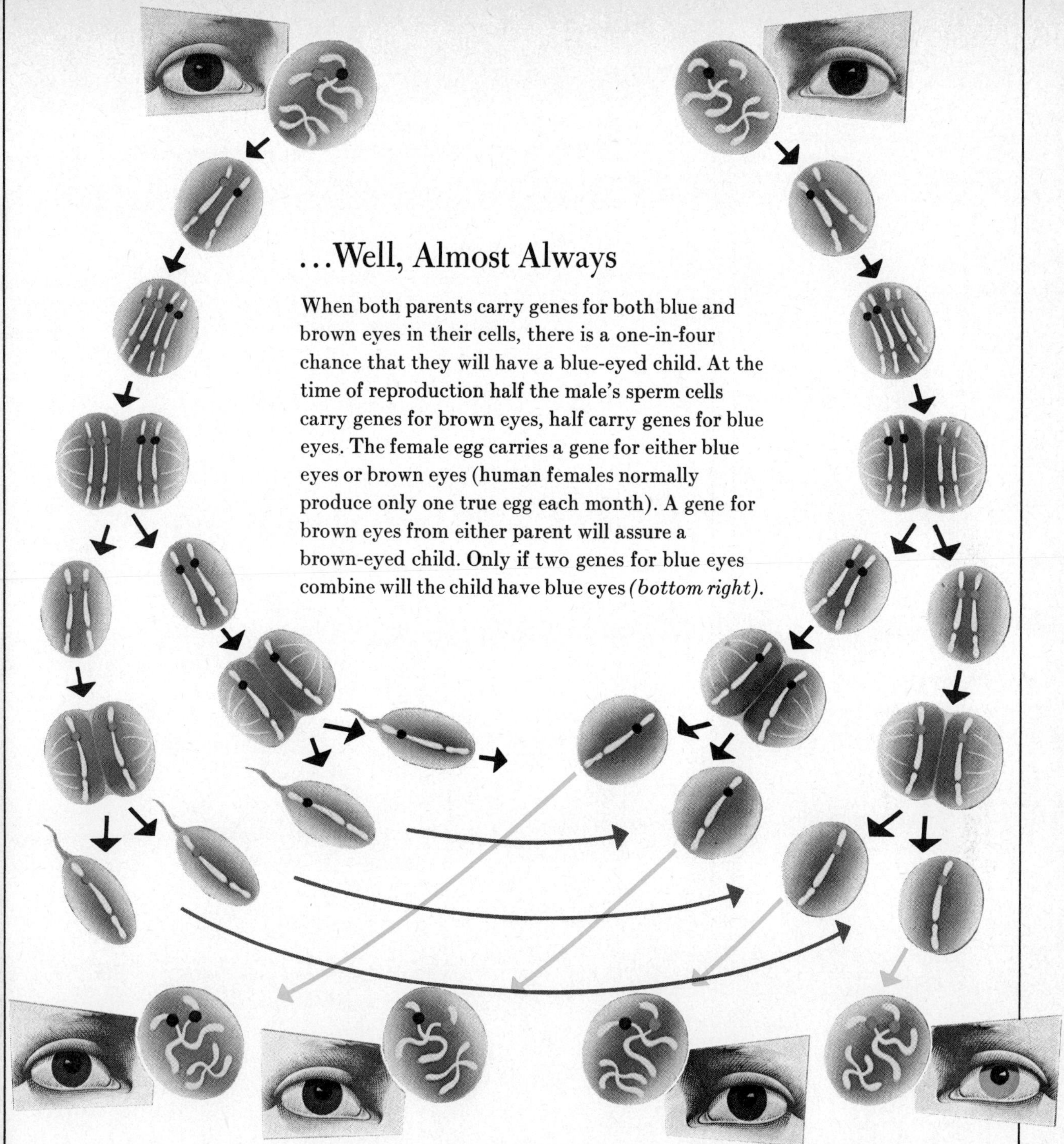

...Well, Almost Always

When both parents carry genes for both blue and brown eyes in their cells, there is a one-in-four chance that they will have a blue-eyed child. At the time of reproduction half the male's sperm cells carry genes for brown eyes, half carry genes for blue eyes. The female egg carries a gene for either blue eyes or brown eyes (human females normally produce only one true egg each month). A gene for brown eyes from either parent will assure a brown-eyed child. Only if two genes for blue eyes combine will the child have blue eyes *(bottom right)*.

hybrids. The next step was to see what characteristics these hybrids might be hiding. To find out, he planned to let the hybrids fertilize themselves in the normal manner of peas. As soon as spring came he planted his hybrid seeds and again waited for results.

Once again the critical time came when the pods could be opened. Mendel broke open the first. Inside lay both round and wrinkled peas, side by side in the same pod! The "lost"

LUNGFISH

RAVEN

wrinkling of the wrinkled grandparent plant had reappeared. Mendel went on to harvest 7,324 peas from his "seed form" garden. Exactly 5,474 of them were round and 1,850 wrinkled. The ratio was nearly three round peas to one wrinkled pea.

But what would happen in the third generation? The next year Mendel planted his three-to-one group and again permitted each plant to fertilize itself. Now the wrinkled seeds produced only wrinkled peas.

The story was remarkably different with the round seeds. In appearance they were identical, but when Mendel planted them, some differences appeared. Two out of three of the plants produced three round peas for each wrinkled pea. One out of three plants bore only round peas. Why did seemingly identical peas produce such varied descendants? With this question, Mendel began to solve the age-old riddle of heredity. The true hereditary nature of the round peas was hidden in their genetic apparatus. Some were

RACCOON

A Lack of Color

All of the animals above are white, or nearly so, because they suffer from a deficiency called albinism. This mutation, or change, is caused by a recessive gene that does not function correctly. The gene is unable to order the body of the animal to produce melanin, a pigment that colors skin, hair and eyes (the eyes of albinos are red because they lack the pigment that in normal creatures masks the tiny blood vessels). Albinism occurs in almost every animal group, including man, where it appears in one out of 20,000 births.

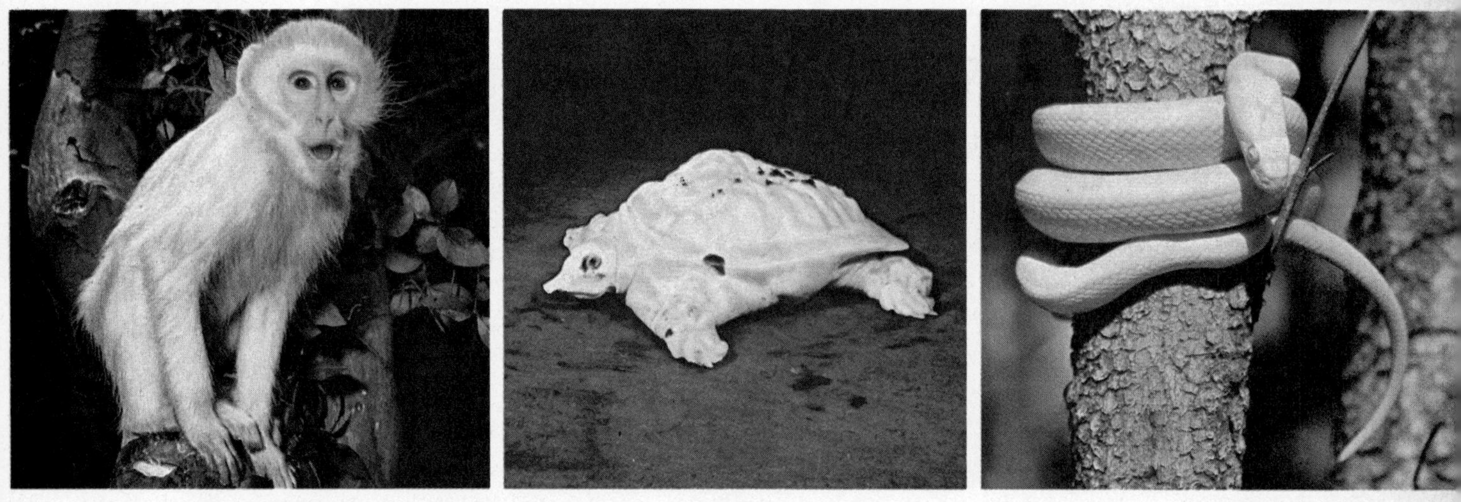

VERVET MONKEY TURTLE RAT SNAKE

truly round and produced only round descendants. Others merely looked round, and produced both wrinkled and round descendants. Which was which could be revealed only by planting them to see what kind of seeds they would produce. This test disclosed that two out of three rounds were actually hybrids; only one of three was a true round.

Mendel labeled the dominant characteristic "A" and the recessive one "a." When A and A came together it meant two dominants (when round-pea pollen fertilized round-pea seeds) and the possibility of nothing but round peas. When a and a came together it meant two recessives and the possibility of nothing but wrinkled peas. It was only when A was combined with a to form Aa that hybrids occurred.

Mendel had concentrated up to this point on single contrasting characteristics. What would happen, he asked, if *two* or more different characteristics were to be united? To see, he crossed round yellow peas with wrinkled green peas. As he anticipated, all the first-generation offspring were round and yellow—both dominant characteristics. But in the next plantings, the round yellows revealed their inner nature. As Mendel broke open the dry pods, he found in some of them four different kinds of peas: round yellow, wrinkled yellow, round green and wrinkled green.

Once again the ratios were almost exactly three to one—three round to one wrinkled, three round yellow to one round green. Mendel proceeded to formulate the biological laws that he saw must underlie his findings:

(1) Heredity is transmitted by a large number of independent, inheritable units.

(2) When each parent contributes the same kind of factor, a constant character is produced in the progeny. If each furnishes a different kind of factor, a hybrid results, and when the hybrid forms its own reproductive cells the two different units "liberate" themselves again to work independently.

(3) The hereditary units are unaffected by their long association with others in an individual. They emerge from any union as distinct as when they entered.

Mendel himself at first regarded his findings only as theories that required further testing. If he was correct though, and each hybrid pea was made up of independent hereditary units, it should be possible to prove the point by a different shuffling of the units.

To test this, Mendel first took a hybrid round-yellow pea seed (AaBb) and formed: AABb, AaBB, AaBb and AABB. Since each combination contained two dominants, all the peas were round and yellow in appearance. Their true nature would emerge on later plantings.

Then Mendel crossed the hybrid AaBb with the recessive aabb, the green wrinkled one. Again four combinations were formed and in almost equal numbers.

All the necessary tests had been made. The results had been predicted and nature had responded with astonishing exactness. The time had come for Mendel to publish a report on his eight years of work. During the fall and winter of 1864 he wrote the paper that would demonstrate for the first time how individual traits or characteristics are transmitted from parent to offspring.

On a frosty night in February 1865 Mendel began to read his paper before a group of natural scientists, who listened in unbroken silence to his discussion of the unvarying ratios in pea hybrids. At the next meeting Mendel went on to explain what the ratios meant. The combination of mathematics and

DESERT FOX

Evolution in Ears

The ears of the foxes at left show one way that animals adapt to their surroundings. Ears help to radiate, or give off, body heat; over a long period of time they have evolved to suit these three species living in different climates. To conserve body heat, the arctic fox has the smallest ears; those of the red fox of the eastern U.S. are medium-sized to get rid of heat. The desert fox has the largest ears, which also help it track down prey in the cool, dark, desert nights.

botany was unheard of; the idea that lay behind it—a vast shuffling of unseeable, unknown units—ran completely contrary to the belief that heredity was a matter of "blood." Nevertheless, Mendel was invited to prepare his paper for publication, and his "Experiments in Plant Hybridization" appeared in 1866. Copies were sent to more than 120 scientific organizations and universities in Europe and America. Once more there was silence. No one praised or disputed Mendel's work, or gave it any attention at all.

Mendel now began to work with beans, and upsetting results began to appear. Only in certain characteristics did the beans' flowers follow the same laws as the peas. When Mendel crossed a white-flowered, white-seeded bean with one having reddish-purple flowers and red seeds flecked with black, all of the first generation bore pale red flowers unlike either parent. In the next hybrid generation Mendel was greeted with a burst of color, from the pure white of one flower through a wide spectrum ending in reddish-purple. He was looking upon some colors that had not previously appeared in any of his test plants.

Could he have been wrong? Could an error have been made in his first results, which had shown that the first hybrid generation resembled the dominant parent? It occurred to Mendel that if the trait of color is determined in some species not by a single hereditary unit but by two such units acting together, then all of the nonconforming results could be explained. The two could produce nine variations of color. Only one ninth of the plants would bear white flowers, and eight ninths would produce almost exactly the range of color he had observed. This indicated that more than one hereditary unit entered into the production of certain traits. Mendel had come upon another of the basic laws of heredity.

In 1868 Mendel was elected abbot of the monastery at Brünn and his experiments had to be dropped entirely. Death came to the abbot on January 6, 1884. Townspeople and authorities gathered for the funeral of the highly respected man. But it was doubtful that anyone in the gathering, or in the world, realized that a great scientist had gone or that his fame would be everlasting. Even his experimental notes and records disappeared.

Darwin had died two years earlier without finding the answer to the problem of evolution. With the passing of the years, the problem became increasingly critical. In the 1880s Hugo de Vries, a botanist at the University of Amsterdam, was one of those asking how the variations and modifications of life come about. De Vries accepted Darwin's thesis that descent with modification is the main law of nature in the organic world. But if natural selection had only small, individual variations to act upon, how could the wide differences between species be produced?

Size Set by Environment

In different areas, animals of the same species differ. The European bear below weighs up to 600 pounds; its Siberian cousin *(outline),* from a cold area with different food, weighs up to 800 pounds.

De Vries knew that breeders could produce only limited changes when they had only individual differences with which to work. By selecting the redder tulips in their gardens they could breed a more intensely red flower. But for a completely different shade of red they had to wait upon nature and its production of what the botanist De Vries called a "mutation."

De Vries decided to watch for the occurrence of mutations. One afternoon in 1886, as he walked through the countryside near Hilversum, a yellow mass of the evening primrose, *Oenothera lamarckiana,* caught his eye. The tall plants with the golden flowers, which had been growing in a nearby park, were now multiplying rapidly in a former potato field. De Vries hurried over to examine them closely, and saw that they varied widely. There were differences in the shape of the leaves, in the height of the plants and in the way they branched.

De Vries decided to make a thorough study of them—and thereby launched one of the most extensive and famous of all plant studies. In the summer of 1887, as he studied the primrose plants, De Vries found 10 specimens of a new type. The 10 were growing by themselves in a corner of the field that had not been invaded by any of the other primroses. Their petals were smaller and more oval than the heart-shaped petals of the *lamarckianas.* Were they truly a new species and would they produce others of their kind? De Vries could not know until he planted their seeds. When he did, they produced new plants with small, oval petals like those of the parent plant and quite unlike the petals of the *lamarckianas.* He felt certain that he had a new species and named it *Oenothera laevifolia.*

During the next decade De Vries raised or observed 53,509 primrose plants. Among them he discovered what he believed to be several new species. As he studied the data from this enormous experiment, De Vries could see a pattern. The new plants always appeared full-blown. He could find no intermediates between the *lamarckianas* and the newcomers. And once the new plant had appeared it went on repeating itself; it did not go back to its ancestral form.

De Vries also noticed that the new plants did not change in all their aspects as he and most naturalists would have expected. There was no over-all alteration.

If plants and other living things changed only at one or a few points, this suggested that the characters must be produced by separate hereditary units. If this were so, De Vries thought, then each part could vary separately.

This was venturing onto new ground, and he tried to find out whether any other naturalist had suggested that heredity was not a whole but a compound of separate units. The search led to Mendel, and in 1900 De Vries discovered the work that the patient Austrian monk had published in 1866. On the basis of his own work, De Vries knew at once the import of what he was reading. Time and

progress had at last caught up with Mendel. Until this moment De Vries had thought that he, and not an unknown monk of an earlier generation, had discovered the long-sought secrets of heredity.

Like Darwin confronted with Wallace's work, De Vries did not hesitate. In a paper read before the German Botanical Society on March 24, 1900, the Dutch botanist gave full credit for one of the most momentous discoveries in scientific history to Mendel. And the theory of evolution at last had its base.

Patterns Made by Man

Evolution under man's control is seen in the gaily colored, orderly flowerbeds of a seed farm in central California. Many new strains are grown here after being developed by scientific breeding of seeds, a modern-day business made possible by Mendel's early interest in crossing flowers and vegetables.

4

Cracking the "Code" of Living Things

A CURIOUS YOUNG LADY takes a good look at a huge model of a DNA molecule. The balls and rods represent the many parts of DNA, which holds the secrets of heredity and controls life. These molecules are present in every human cell and in the cells of all plants and animals as well.

A million animal species and a quarter million kinds of plants inhabit the world today. Yet they are only a fraction of the species that have existed, for millions of others have died out. Darwin gave them all a common ancestry. Mendel found that law, not luck, governs their descent. But Darwin and Mendel raised more questions for the 20th Century than they answered for the 19th. What kinds of genetic factors produced all the differences in the forms of life? Where were they hidden away in living tissues? How did they work? Could man ever control them? The search for the answers has brought science close to the deepest secrets of life, and has raised a great deal of argument among scientists.

It seemed to De Vries, the primrose expert, that evolution could never get anywhere by natural selection alone. To him the sudden changes he called mutations were the chief force in pushing things along. He argued that different kinds of things—mutants—have to be present before a selection can be made.

To Darwinians, however, natural, gradual selection was everything, and the large, sudden mutations in species were meaningless in evolution's long run. The battle became

How One Cell Becomes Two

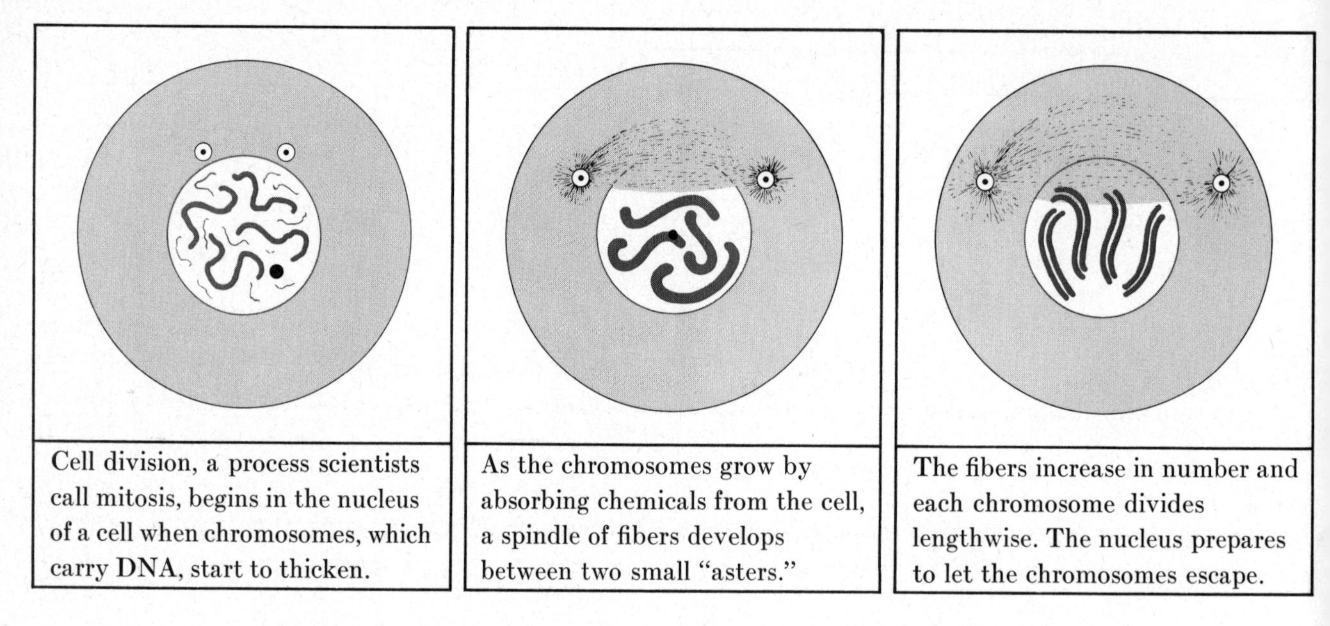

Cell division, a process scientists call mitosis, begins in the nucleus of a cell when chromosomes, which carry DNA, start to thicken.

As the chromosomes grow by absorbing chemicals from the cell, a spindle of fibers develops between two small "asters."

The fibers increase in number and each chromosome divides lengthwise. The nucleus prepares to let the chromosomes escape.

fierce. But finally mutation tumbled from the place De Vries had given it as evolution's chief agent. Natural selection won out, and mutation was given a secondary role as the agent that supplied the raw material for evolutionary changes. Without mutations, nature would sink into a rut. It would be unprepared to cope with such constant changes in physical environment as ice ages, long periods without rain and the slow rise and fall of the earth's crust, or such changes in the living environment as the appearance of a swifter foe, or a deadlier germ.

Reasonable as this analysis was, experiments in many laboratories were showing that most mutations are harmful and the most drastic ones are usually fatal. Most bearers of radical mutations never live long enough to pass the changes along to offspring.

A few small changes, however, can prove helpful to a species. So the next question for the scientists was: how can a rare, tiny, helpful change—say a change in bone structure that makes a fin of a fish potentially usable as a leg—spread through a large species? Will it not be lost in the ordinary mating of two individuals and their descendants?

Not at all, said the mathematicians. Let us consider a mutation that would have an advantage for survival of only 1 per cent over the organism from which it arose. A percentage that small would mean the survival of 100 mutants as against 99 unmutated individuals. This means that the mutant would eventually far outnumber the original.

Furthermore, Sir Ronald Aylmer Fisher, a British mathematician, pointed out that the great contrast between abundant species and rare ones lay in the fact that an

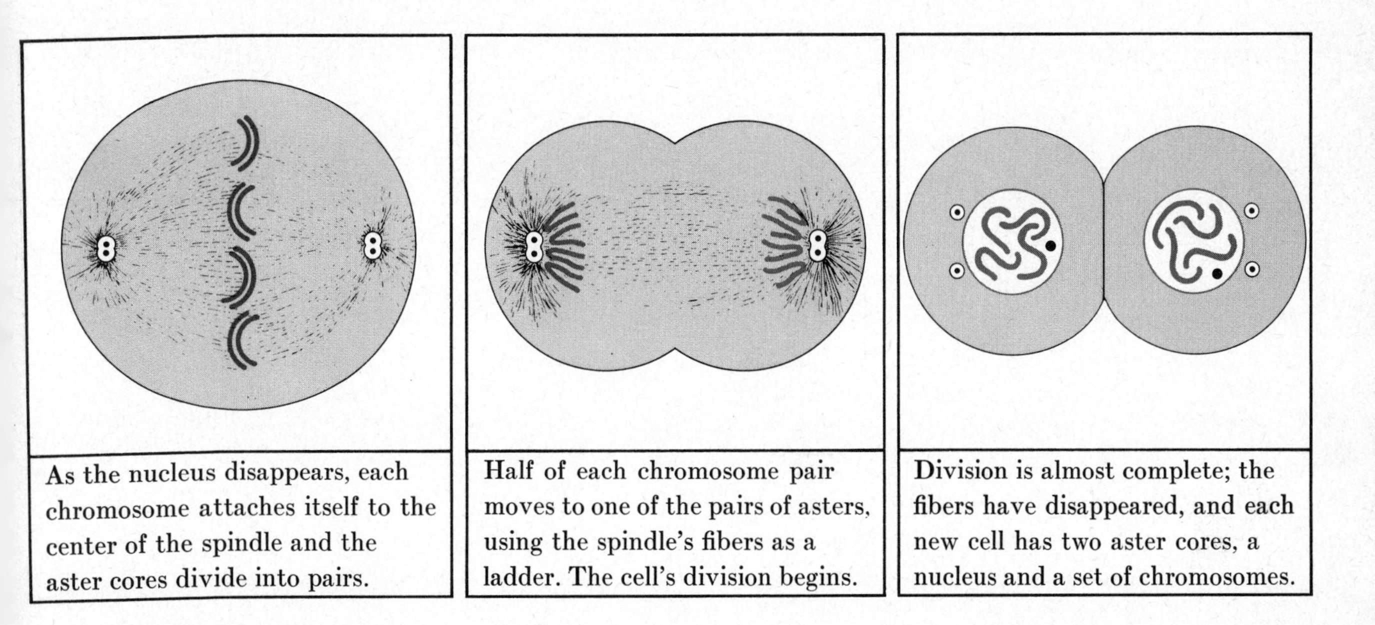

As the nucleus disappears, each chromosome attaches itself to the center of the spindle and the aster cores divide into pairs.

Half of each chromosome pair moves to one of the pairs of asters, using the spindle's fibers as a ladder. The cell's division begins.

Division is almost complete; the fibers have disappeared, and each new cell has two aster cores, a nucleus and a set of chromosomes.

abundance of individuals meant an abundance of possible mutations—hence more possibilities for adapting to new conditions. With fewer possible mutants to help it adapt to changes in the environment, a small species might face a dim future. But a numerous species, such as man, was likely to have a varied enough genetic "pool" to meet almost any change that might confront it. If a species had only 100 characteristics (such as color) that could exist in two forms (yellow or green) he figured, more than 1,000,000,000,000,000,-000,000,000,000,000 genetic combinations were possible when two of its members produced offspring.

Fisher also proved that this richness of variety is directly related to fitness for survival. What counted was not the plant struggling against dry weather or the rabbit escaping the fox, but the nature and the preservation of the material, or units, within them that made it possible for the plant species or the rabbit species to win out. Evolution really concerned the mysterious, almost infinitely changeable units whose existence Mendel had inferred in his experiments with the heredity of plants.

Mendel had had no way to inquire into what such units might be, or where they might be located within the living cell. But in the years when his reports were sitting unread on library shelves, scientists discovered a number of tiny threadlike structures in the nucleus of the cell. When stained with dye, these structures, called chromosomes, could be seen under a microscope.

Close observation revealed that there were actually pairs of chromosomes, and that they went through remarkable maneuvers.

When a normal body cell was about to divide, each chromosome of each pair duplicated itself. The original and its copy then split in two and moved out to opposite ends of the cell. A cell wall grew between them, and in an hour, more or less, there were two cells where there had been only one. Each was equipped with a full, identical set of these chromosome threads.

But when a new egg or sperm cell was to be formed, the maneuvers differed. Only half of each set of the chromosome pairs went into each new reproductive cell. When a male reproductive cell joined a female reproductive cell, the full chromosome number was restored, half of it coming from each parent.

Could chromosomes contain Mendel's hereditary units? In their action they seemed to explain Mendel's findings that hereditary traits paired up in seeds but kept their own independence, in the same way that two marbles may be put together in a bag but remain separate marbles. Chromosome action also supplied the kind of mechanism needed to produce Mendel's many varieties by bringing together half the traits of one hybrid and half the traits of its "mate."

Soon scientists found through experiments that certain traits seemed to be coupled—perhaps controlled by one chromosome.

Thomas Hunt Morgan of Columbia University was one of those who found this kind of coupling. It kept cropping up in the fruit flies, *Drosophila melanogaster,* with which he was working. In 1910, about a year after he began studying the little flies that orbit around ripe fruit, a fly with white eyes appeared in one of the milk bottles he used for incubators. Since the wild flies have red eyes, he felt certain that this was a mutation.

He bred the white-eyed male to a red-eyed female and in a short time had hundreds of red-eyed offspring. To bring out their underlying heredity, Morgan then bred red-eyed hybrids to red-eyed hybrids. The matings produced 50 per cent red-eyed females, 25 per cent red-eyed males, 25 per cent white-eyed males—but not one white-eyed female. By all indications the hereditary unit for white eyes, the mutated unit, was linked to the sex chromosome—assuming of course that the chromosomes were in fact the bearers of heredity. It was obvious to Morgan that if chromosomes really did bear hereditary units, all factors carried by the same chromosome would tend to remain together.

It so happened that the fruit fly had four pairs of chromosomes. If Morgan was right, it should be possible to "map" the hereditary factors carried by each, and he set out to do it. It took nearly 17 years and the breeding of millions of flies, but in the end Morgan and the "fly squad" of young scientists working with him found that there were very precise locations on the chromosomes that controlled such fly characteristics as the shape of the wing and the color of the body. Actual chromosome maps were made: long vertical lines on which were marked the sites of "yellow body, white eyes, echinus eyes, cross veinless, cut wing, vermilion eyes, miniature wing,

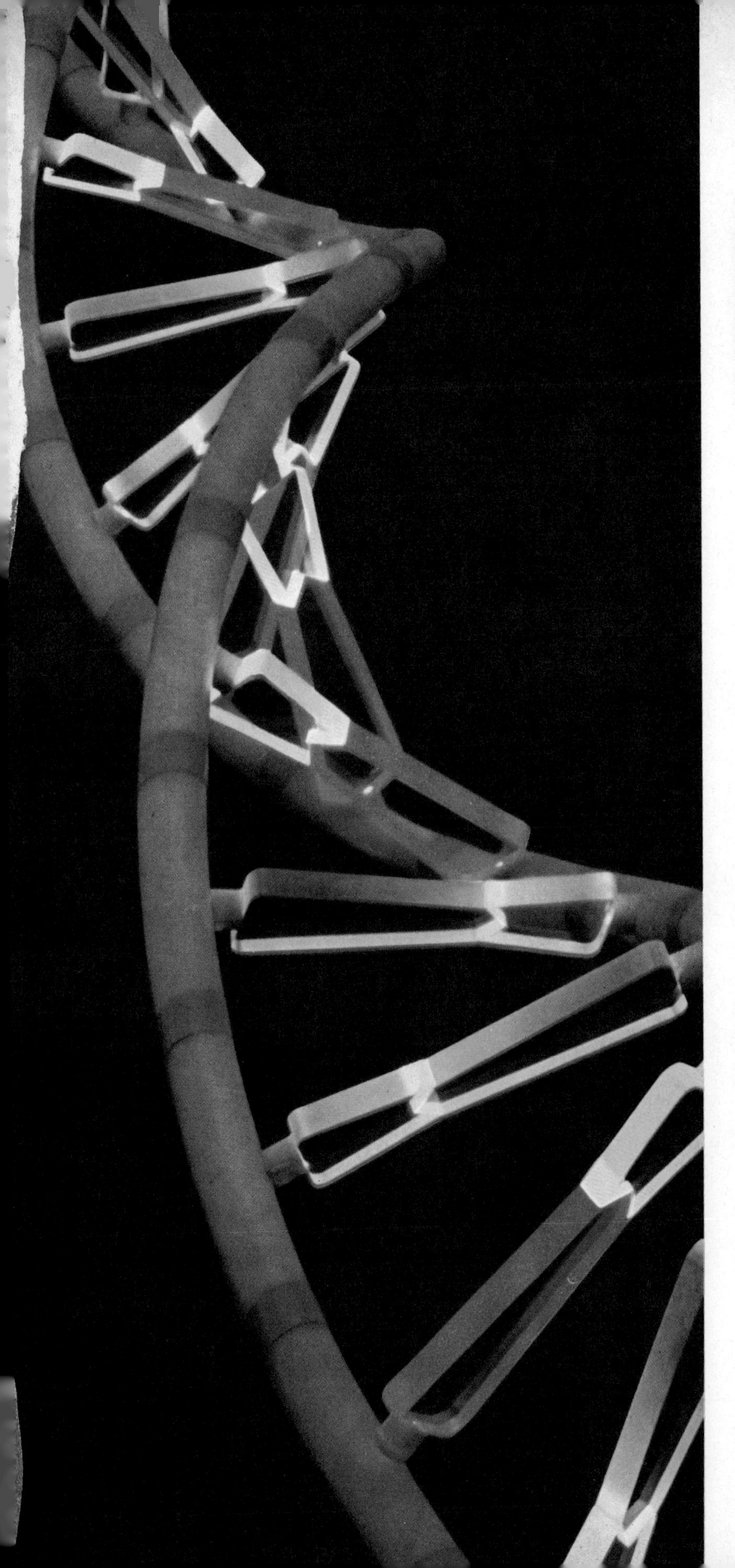

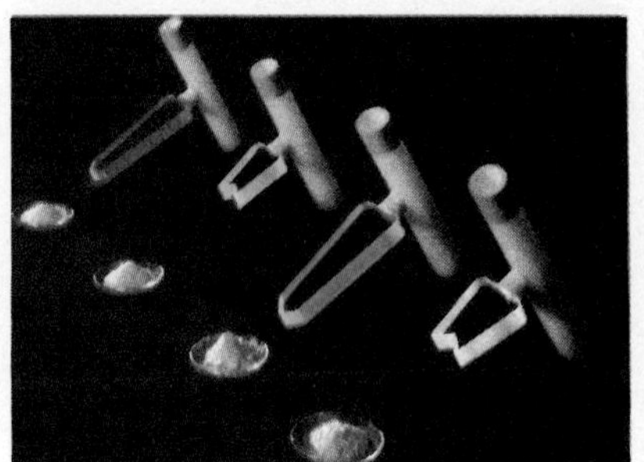

The Basic Rungs of the DNA Ladder

A DNA molecule is composed of nucleotides. These are chemical combinations of phosphate, sugar and one of four bases, shown above by four colored symbols that point to tiny dishes of the actual chemical. The bases always join in the same way: adenine *(red)* with thymine *(green)*; guanine *(blue)* with cytosine *(yellow)*. Once joined, the bases become the "steps" of DNA's staircase, between two sugar-phosphate bands *(left)*.

The Reproduction of DNA

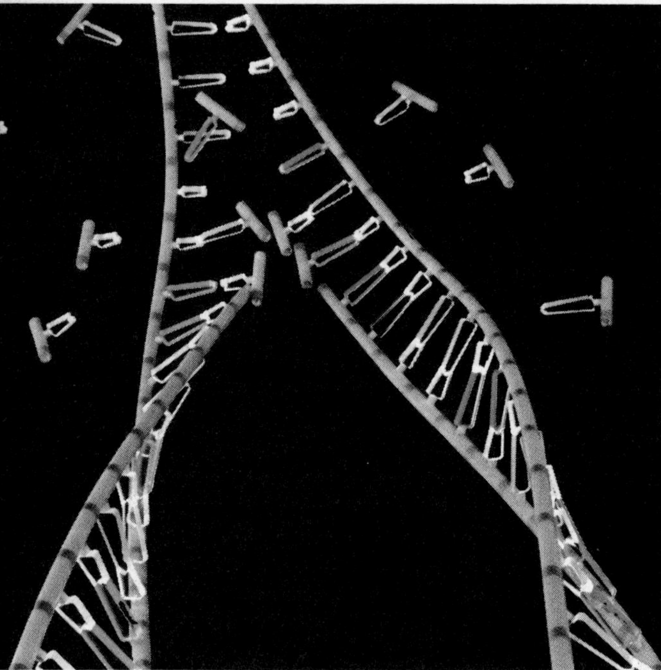

DNA REPEATS ITSELF in a cell as the cell divides. Reproduction begins when two joined bases pull apart, "unzipping" the molecule down the middle *(above)*. Now free-floating nucleotides move to the divided strands.

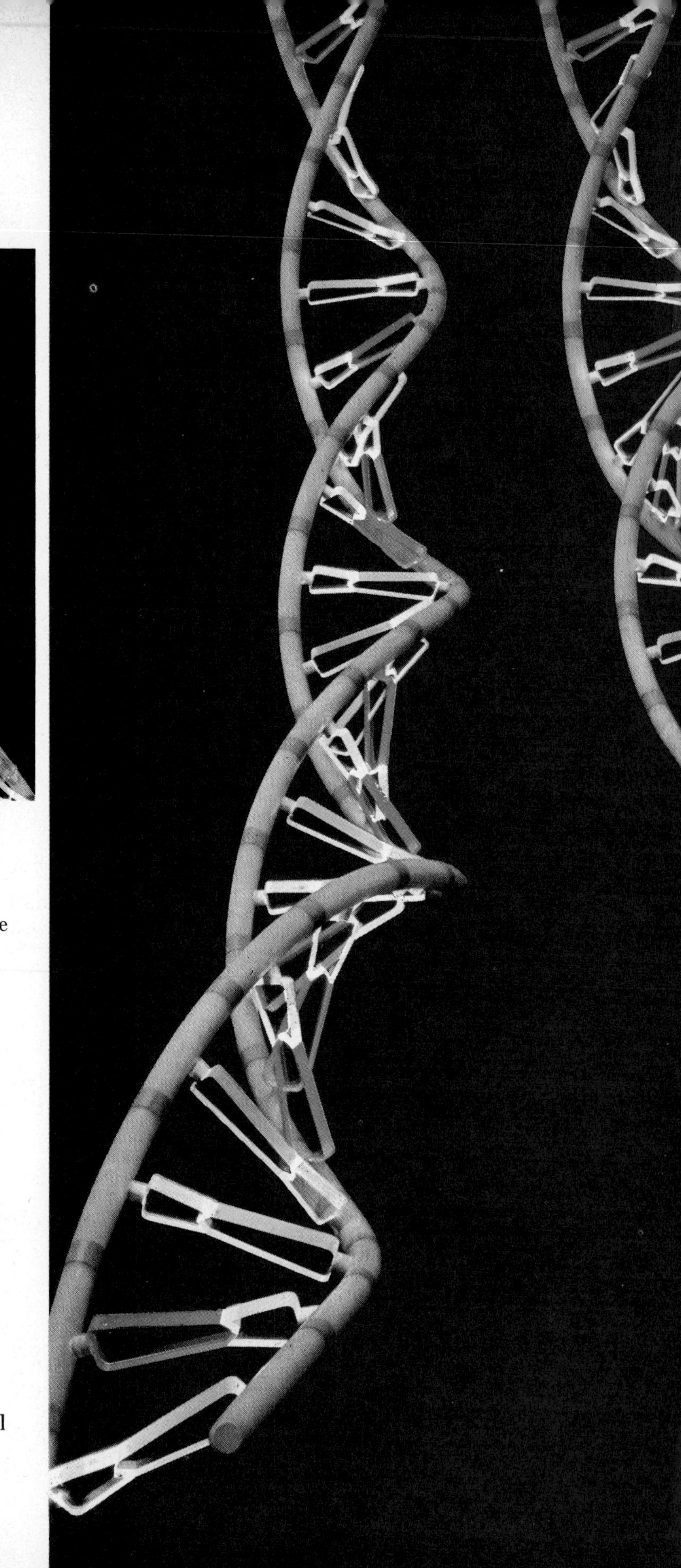

TWO DNA'S FROM ONE result after each base on the two split strands has linked with a base unit exactly like its former partner *(right)*. Continuing the process, each offspring, which is identical to the parent, can now reproduce itself.

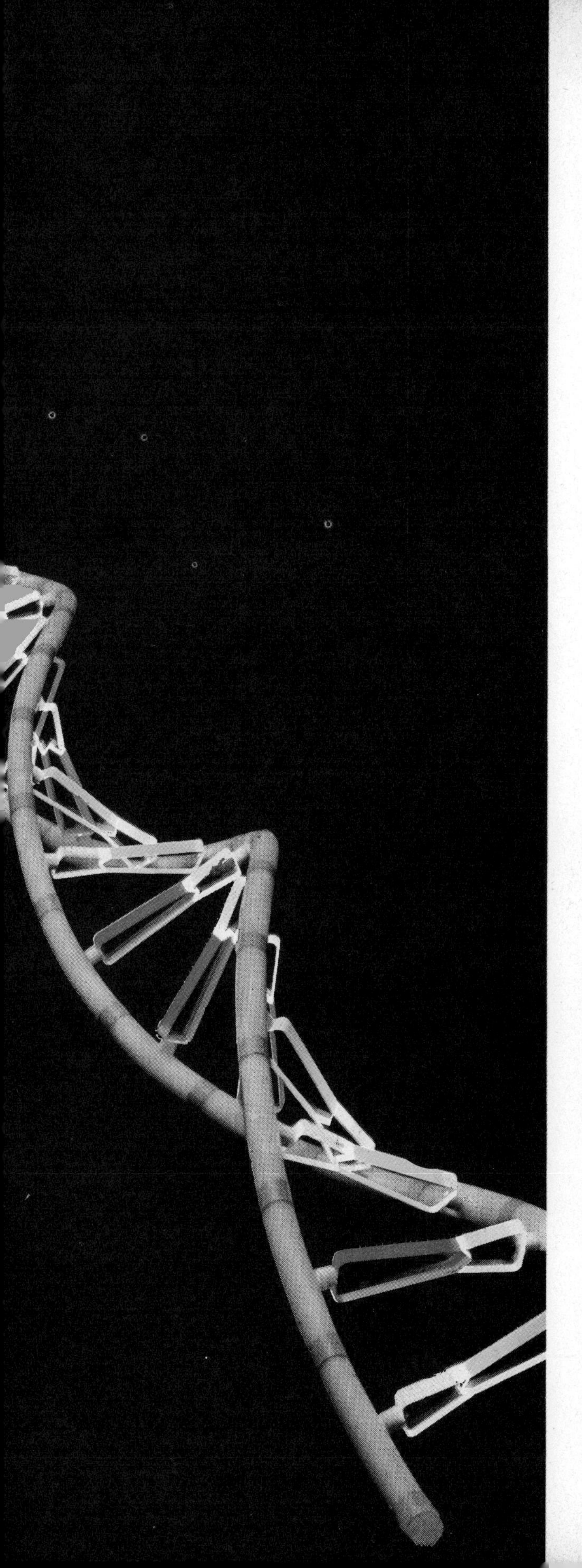

sable body, garnet eyes, forked bristles, bar eyes, clipped wing and bobbed bristles." These were the descriptive names for the different physical characteristics that were determined by the units of a chromosome. These units were given the name genes.

In all the research projects, two most important things were established. One was that inheritance operates through the passing on of separate bits of self-producing matter. The other was that the genes combine or interact to produce their effects, and they are all organized to work as a single system.

But all the same, what *was* a gene, and what happened when a gene mutated? If mutations could be purposely made to happen and their changes were studied, something might be learned about how these bits of self-reproducing matter worked. Many scientists became interested in the problem. In efforts to force changes deep within the nucleus of the cell, they tried heat, cold, drugs, poison and even mutilation. But genes were too tough and stable to be altered by such tampering. Then H. J. Muller, who had begun his scientific work as one of Morgan's "fly squad," got to wondering if mutation might be brought about by ultramicroscopic forces. X-rays, he knew, are capable of striking one minute point with drastic effect while missing another point a thousandth of a millimeter away.

So Muller put hundreds of fruit flies in gelatin capsules and bombarded them with X-rays. These flies were then bred to untreated

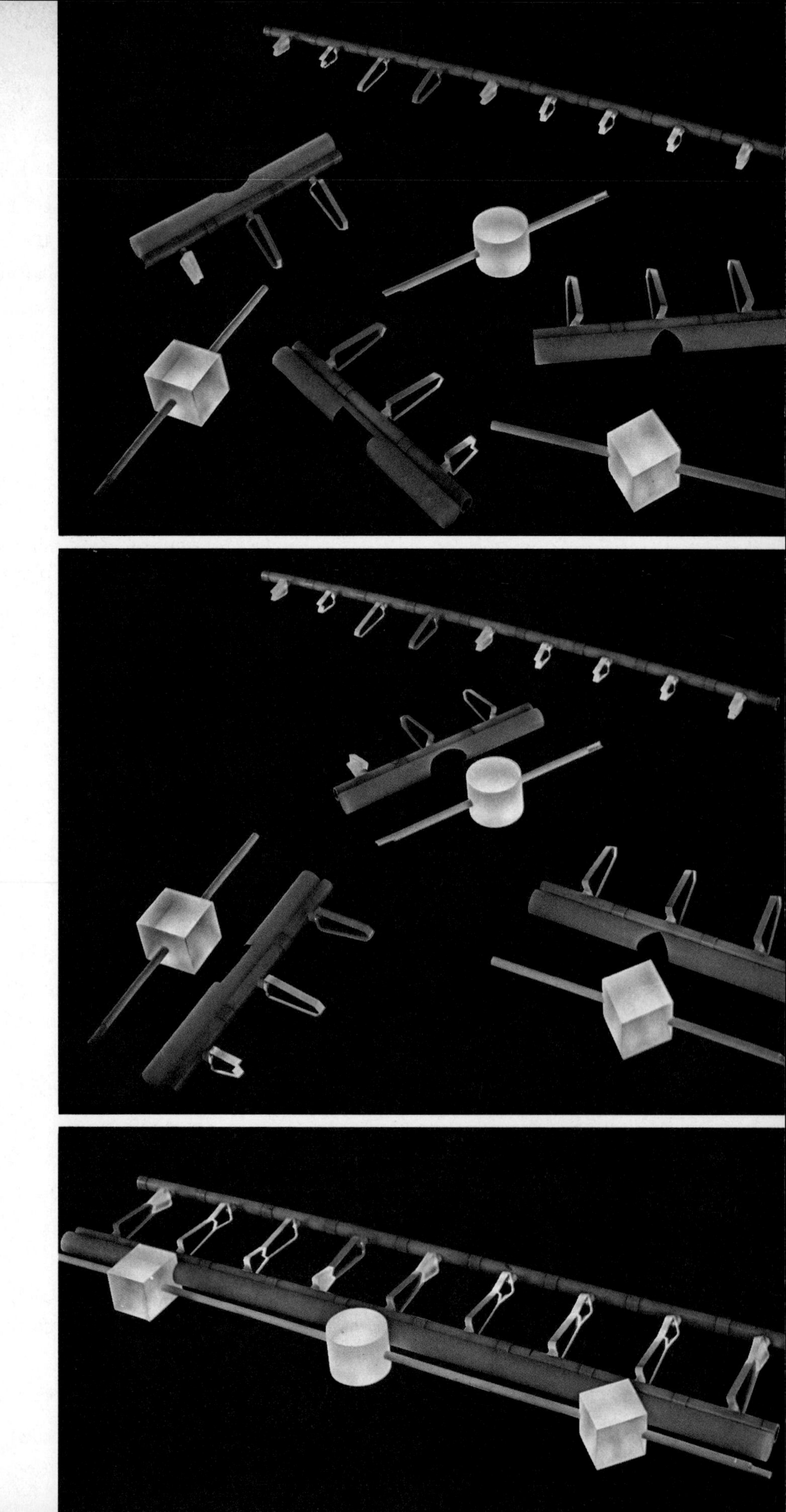

How Protein Is Formed

DNA MAKES RNA, its near-relative, out of floating nucleotides while its strands are "unzipped." RNA helps produce protein, which all organisms need for life. At left, two types of RNA are represented: "messenger" *(top)* and "transfer" *(shorter strands).*

TRANSFER-RNA CAPTURES amino acids *(large cylinders and cubes)* by chemical attraction, symbolized at the left by the different-shaped notches in the backbones of the transfer-RNA molecules. Amino acids are the raw materials of protein.

PROTEINS ARE FORMED as the strip of messenger-RNA becomes an assembly line for transfer-RNAs. As these molecules hitch on to the messenger-RNA in the precise sequence that DNA had originally dictated, amino acids link to form a protein molecule.

ones. In 10 days thousands of their offspring were buzzing around their banana-mash feed, and Muller was looking upon an unequalled outburst of man-made mutations.

There were flies with bulging eyes, flat eyes, purple, yellow and brown eyes. Some had curly bristles, some no bristles. There were flies with broad wings or downturned wings or almost no wings at all. "They were a motley throng," said Muller. "The results of these experiments were startling. . . . The roots of life—the genes—had indeed been struck and they had yielded." Muller's work in the field of genetics won him a Nobel Prize, the most famous prize for scientific achievement in the world.

Although the genes had told Muller and others some secrets of their mechanics, their chemistry remained a mystery. Through most of the years while Mendel and Morgan were tracing the effects of heredity's units, and while others were showing that the whole theory of evolution was based on genes and the way they changed and recombined continuously, bottles of a white powder were sitting on the shelves of many laboratories. This powder was labeled nucleic acid.

A Swiss chemist named Friedrich Miescher had discovered this acid in 1869 while breaking down some cells. The cells broke up as expected but part of each center, or nucleus, remained intact. When this remainder was analyzed, it was found to differ chemically from all other known material that appears in cells.

In time other scientists found that the acid

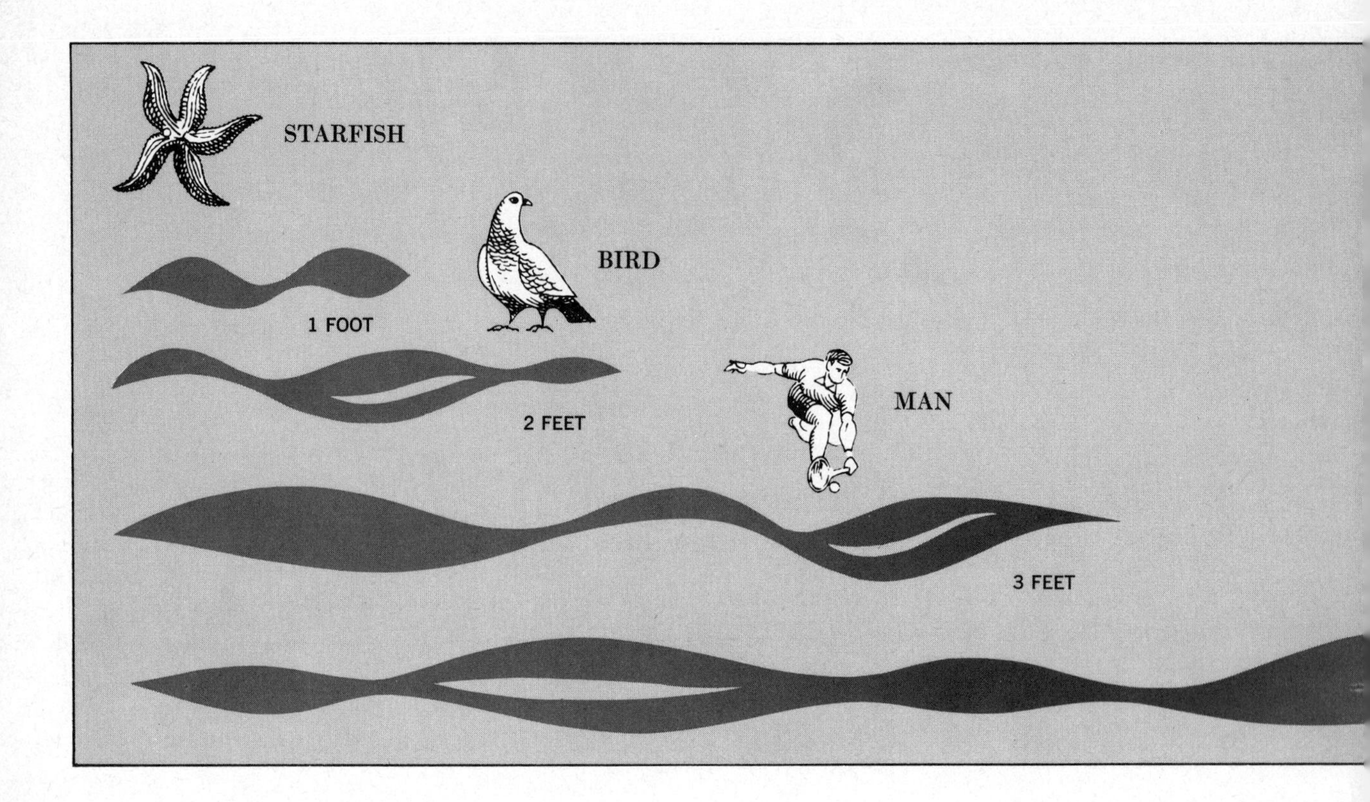

was composed of huge molecules. They also learned that nucleic acid was found only in chromosomes. Its chemical composition was worked out and the powder was renamed deoxyribonucleic acid, or DNA for short. Later a second nucleic acid was found that differed only slightly from DNA. It was called RNA, for ribonucleic acid. There the matter rested; the bottles continued to sit on laboratory shelves.

By the 1940s it was clear that the answer for the form and functioning of life had to be sought in the materials out of which chromosomes were made. These were essentially two, DNA and protein. Between 1941 and 1944 three scientists at the Rockefeller Institute in New York City found that DNA carried genes and therefore directed heredity.

DNA had been neglected for so long, however, that it was hard for scientists to accept this finding. But in 1952, firm proof came. A brilliant series of experiments at the Biological Laboratory in Cold Spring Harbor, New York, showed that when a virus, acting much like a physician's syringe, shot its DNA contents into a bacterial cell, the DNA took command and in 24 minutes produced complete copies of itself. The virus's protein shell, comparable to the casing of the syringe, had been left on the outside of the cell wall. All that entered the cell was the DNA, and it produced not only new DNA but new protein "overcoats" for the new viruses as well. The

The Long and Short of DNA

Scientists have measured the lengths of DNA strips in different kinds of living things and have found that the strips usually get longer as creatures become more complex. However, there are startling exceptions. If the coiled strips of DNA in one human cell could be teased out to full length and placed end to end, they would make a thread about three feet long. But the DNA strips from the cell of a frog have a total length of eight feet, more than twice that of the strips from a man's cell.

raw material of heredity, the basic stuff of life and evoluton, had at last been found.

Here, lying in a cell, was a bit of matter too small to be seen except with the tremendous enlarging power of the electron microscope. Yet this bit of matter held all the instruction needed for the building of a virus or a beetle—or a man. Its composition was simple enough. All DNA is made of nucleotides, which are chemical combinations of sugar, phosphate and one of four nitrogen bases: adenine, thymine, cytosine and guanine (known as A, T, C, and G.) Obviously with only these four nucleotides involved, the secret of DNA's ability to issue instructions had to rest in the endless number of ways, or sequences, in which they could be put together to form different living things.

In the 1950s the trackdown of this secret began in laboratories all over the world. At the Cavendish Laboratory at Cambridge, England, Francis H. C. Crick, a British physicist-turned-biologist, and James D. Watson, a young American biologist, fashioned a wire model that portrayed a DNA molecule looking like a spiral staircase. The sugar and the phosphate were the framework; the four bases, A, T, C, and G, were linked together—A always with T, C with G—and strung between the framework like steps.

A single gene on a chromosome might be composed of 2,000 such steps. The 46 chromosomes in a human being contain a total of four to six billion steps, and if each of these was written down as a single alphabetical letter, the total would fill 100 dictionaries.

This grand, almost unbelievably complex, staircase keeps life going in two ways: it reproduces itself, and it manufactures protein that cells need in order to function properly. DNA duplicates itself in a remarkable, well-ordered way as the cells in a living organism multiply. The process begins when the two halves of each step pull apart or "unzip." Each half makes itself whole again by picking up appropriate free-floating nucleotides that are present in the cell's nucleus. Thus a T base along the chain will again attract a free A base.

In order to supervise the production of protein, DNA sends out a tremendous number of instructions. There are an estimated 100,000 different kinds of proteins in the human body alone. (Many of these are enzymes, which speed up chemical reactions in the cell and keep it hustling during its brief lifespan.)

It may seem strange that the body must manufacture protein when we consume it in food that comes from plants and plant-eating animals. However, food protein has to be converted into smaller units called amino acids before it can be carried through our bloodstream to the cells. Once there, amino acids are in turn the raw material for body protein. Therefore, DNA deals with amino acids, which are, curiously, composed of almost the same nitrogen bases that are present in DNA's nucleotides.

One of the first clues to the relationships between DNA and amino acids came about quite accidentally. At a dinner of scientists, a physician fell to discussing sickle-cell anemia, a disease of the red cells in human blood. When blood is on its way back to the heart, it is low in oxygen, having dropped off its load to all parts of the body. In sickle-cell anemia, this low amount of oxygen may cause a cell to become shaped like a sickle, a curving blade that looks something like a boomerang. When the blood passes through the lungs and picks up oxygen again, the cells may resume their normal round form. Or, if the anemia is severe, the red cells may rupture in the capillaries. A person who inherits a high percentage of sickle cells gets a serious anemia that is sometimes fatal.

Linus Pauling, a Nobel Prize winner at the California Institute of Technology, listened to all this with excitement. He was not familiar with sickle-cell anemia, but as a chemist he knew that the only parts of the red cells that are concerned with the regular taking on and giving up of oxygen are protein molecules called hemoglobin—100 million of them to a cell. He suspected that the disease would

Mixing Up DNA's Orders

DNA makes uncountable numbers of exact copies of itself as it directs our lives, but its pattern may be altered by attacks from such external forces as radiation. If a cosmic ray *(diagonal streak in model at right)* should strike DNA and disrupt it, its coded orders to growing cells could be garbled.

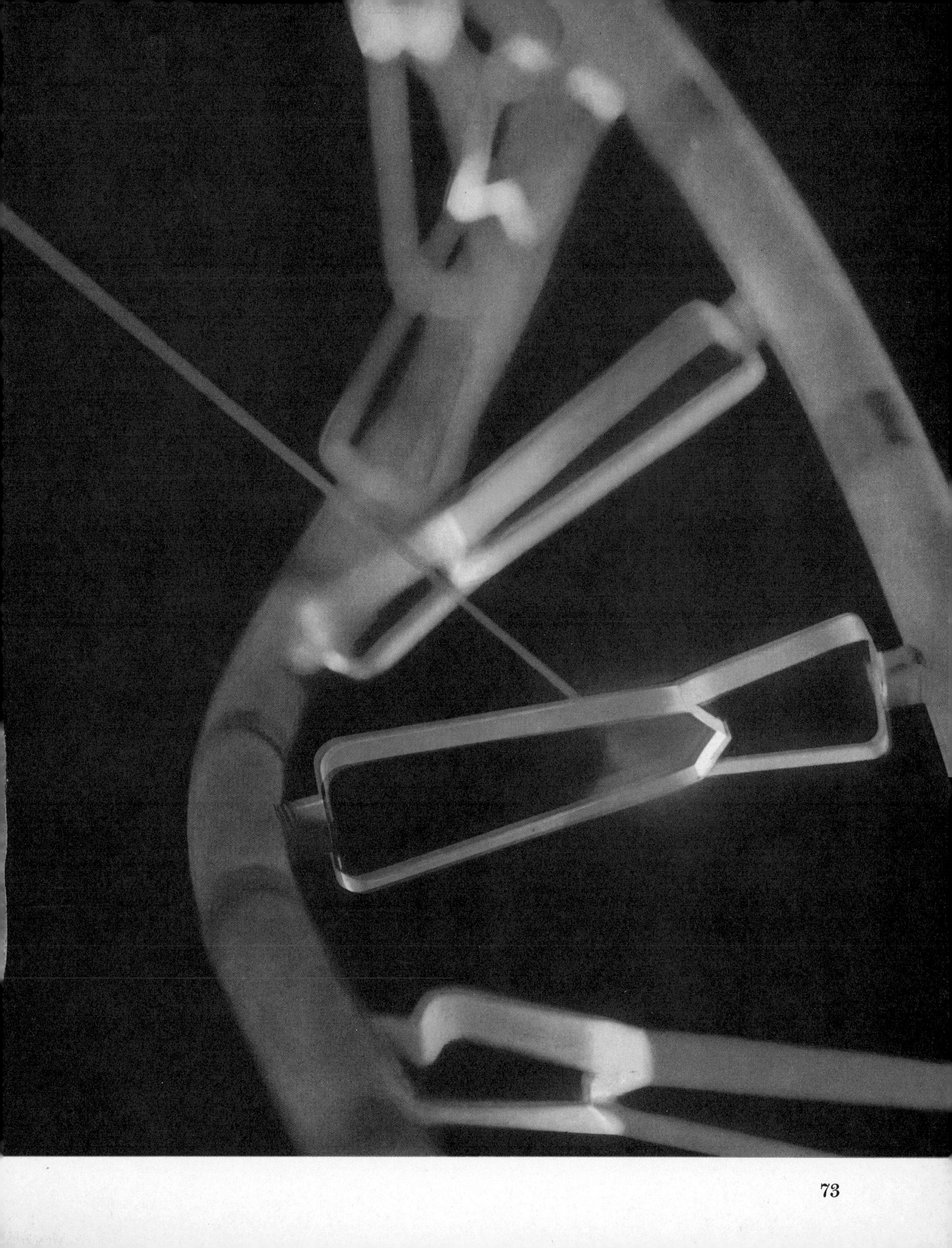

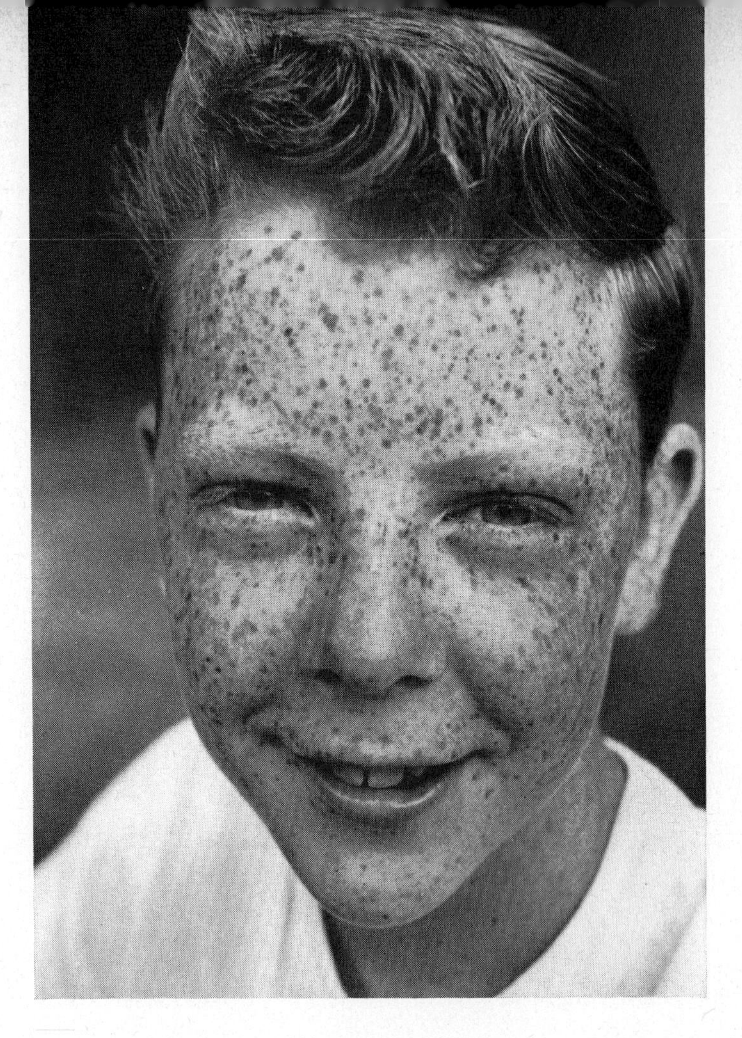

Trademarks of Heredity

The boy's freckles and the woman's tongue-rolling in the pictures at the right are both traits that have been inherited. The boy can be sure that one of his parents and one of his grandparents had freckles too, for this is a dominant trait that reappears in one generation after another. The way this woman curls her tongue is also due to a dominant gene (seven of 10 people can do it), but the ability to fold the tongue's tip back into the mouth is recessive and hence extremely rare.

occur if the genes that control the manufacture of hemoglobin were abnormal.

Pauling's insight proved correct. Vernon M. Ingram of Cambridge University decided to trace the sickle-cell disease back to its DNA source, in other words, to the arrangement of DNA bases in the abnormal genes producing this disease. By breaking up a sickle-cell hemoglobin molecule and a normal one and comparing them, Ingram learned that they differed only at one point, which he called the "Number Four spot." This spot in normal cells includes two units of glutamic acid and one of valine, both amino acids. The sickle-cells include the reverse, one unit of glutamic acid and two of valine.

At this point the scientists had to theorize in part. Assuming that DNA was organized in the spiral-staircase form, Ingram and his associate John Hunt drew up a diagram showing how the four nucleotide bases, A, T, C, and G, might be arranged in one section in order to get the normal amino acid—glutamic—for the normal hemoglobin. It read like this:

C———G
T———A
G———C

But if a mutation replaced that T———A pairing with a G———C pairing, the mutated line-up would be:

C———G
G———C
G———C

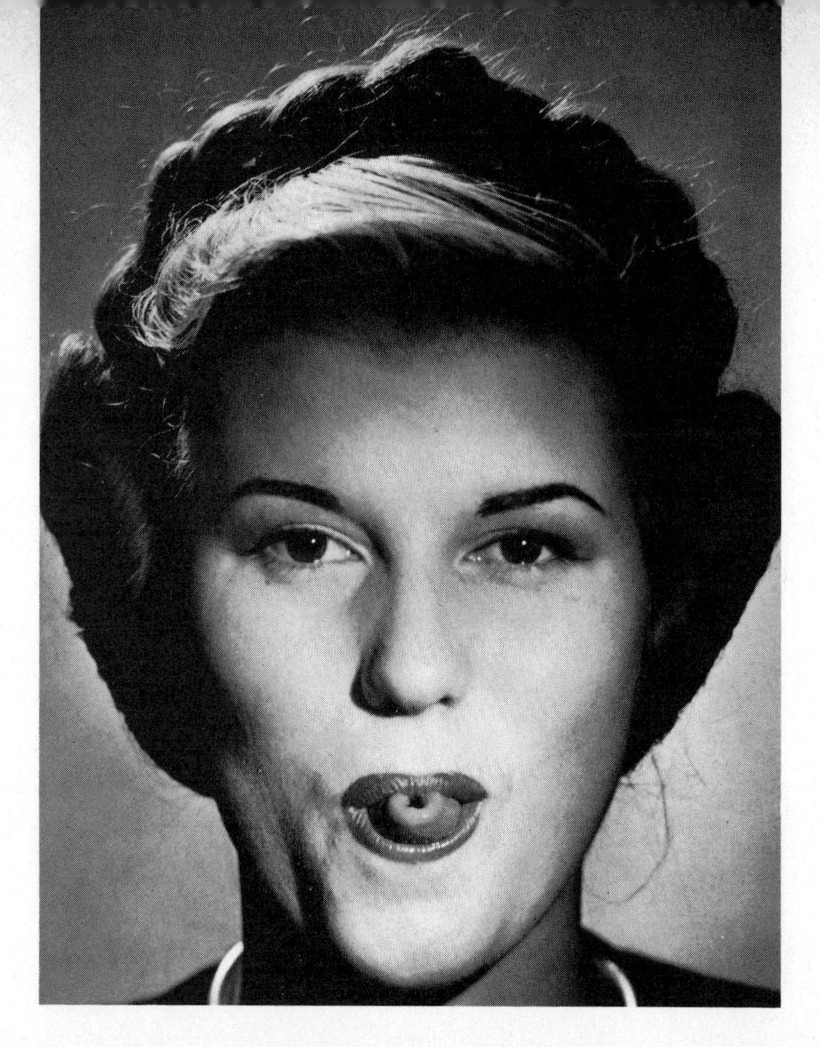

and valine would result. The latter is exactly the amino acid that, in this spot, causes sickle-cell anemia.

A mutation in DNA thus may be a change in a single nucleotide, or "step." In greatly simplified terms it is the line-up of the DNA, whether normal or mutated, that dictates the order of amino acids in the protein; this in turn dictates the "shape" of the protein and the forms of all living things. Or to put it into numbers, the four bases of DNA arrange 20 universal amino acids in patterns forming the thousands of proteins that control life's infinite variety.

Now scientists could draw up a code indicating how the four "steps" could assemble the 20 universal amino acids, but until 1961 the code was purely theoretical. Then Marshall Nirenberg of the National Institutes of Health broke the code for one amino acid. He was working with RNA, which is a near-replica of DNA, and which moves out of the cell nucleus into the cell's outer part to do the actual work of producing proteins. DNA, like an architect's master plan, is preserved and guarded, while RNA, like a blueprint, is used for the everyday work. Since that time Nirenberg, Severo Ochoa of New York University and others have figured out the line-up for all 20.

These arrangements, a sequence of "triplets" (every triplet containing three pairs of linked bases) constitute heredity's all-im-

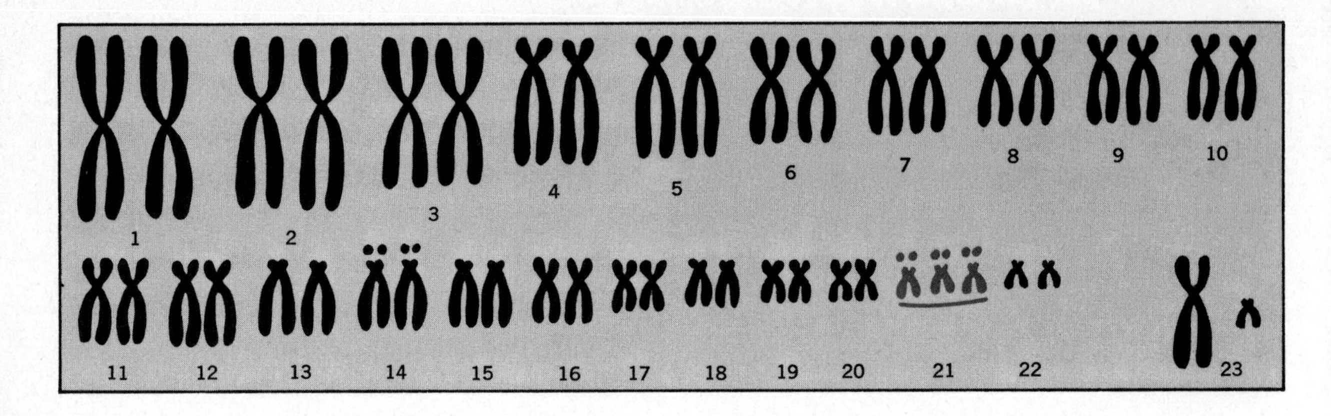

A Mistake Chromosomes Make

An abnormal arrangement of chromosomes sometimes occurs in humans and usually causes grave defects, present at birth. Diagrammed above is the irregular grouping of chromosomes that produces Down's disease. Instead of the normal 23 pairs of chromosomes, this group has a 21st cluster with three chromosomes. A child born with this defect is usually mentally retarded.

portant genetic code. It is the oldest language in the world by far, for scientists are discovering that the same triplets of bases will produce the same amino acids in any species, including the lowest bacteria that first appeared on earth at least two billion years ago.

An experiment showing that all of life is assembled by one process was performed in 1962 at the Rockefeller Institute by Dr. Fritz Lipmann. Another Nobel Prize winner, Dr. Lipmann and his group of associates took RNA from a bacteria found in human intestines and used it to create rabbit hemoglobin. Here was genetic material from bacteria, operating to make the blood of an animal. It hardly would be more amazing for a cat to give birth to a fish, or a plant to puppies.

Why indeed doesn't a geranium plant bear puppies? The DNA molecules of geraniums and puppies do contain the same ingredients. But the lengths and arrangements of DNA in each creature are not the same. Because these differences are unique to each kind of living thing, geraniums bear geranium flowers, and puppies are born only to dogs.

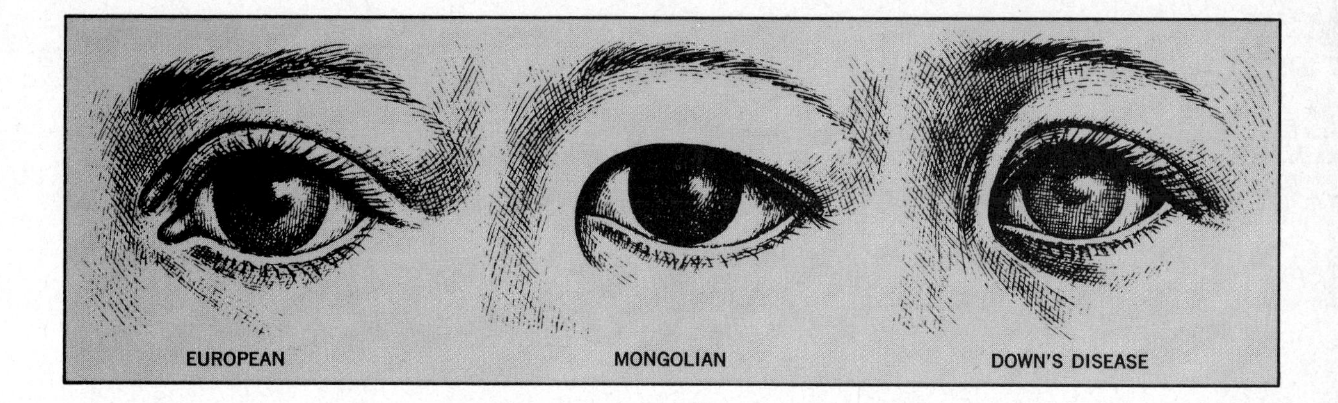

A Telltale Eyefold

Down's disease, caused by the abnormal arrangement of chromosomes like that on the opposite page, is often called "Mongolism" because the victims' eyes somewhat resemble those of Mongolians, who have a curved, overlapping eyelid *(center)*. A child with Down's disease has a skin fold at the inner corner of the eye *(right)*, but otherwise his eye is like the eye of any European *(left)*.

Within each individual, however, DNA is always the same. The DNA in the cell of a man's muscle is identical to the DNA in his brain cells. How then are brain cells tailored to perform exclusively as brain cells, muscle cells as muscle cells, liver cells as liver cells? Scientists have now learned that another group of proteins, called histones, do this job. The histones cover or uncover genes on the DNA molecule. The covered genes cannot control protein manufacture; the uncovered ones can. In other words, muscle cells are ordered to be made by DNA that has only its muscle-making genes uncovered.

Such discoveries are made continuously, but many questions remain to be answered. One way to learn more about unsolved mysteries is to produce DNA synthetically in the laboratory. Dr. Arthur Kornberg, now at Stanford University, is one biochemist who has done just this. In 1957 he assembled the four nucleotides into an exact replica of a natural piece of DNA. He in effect deciphered the line-up of one tiny, though complex, coil of DNA. For this momentous work he shared the 1959 Nobel Prize in Physiology and Medicine with Dr. Severo Ochoa, who had produced RNA synthetically.

Dr. Kornberg's artificial DNA, however, lacked one basic property of life: it could not reproduce itself as natural DNA does. He and his associates then refined the enzyme that helps DNA perform its feats. Again the scientists took a bit of natural DNA and put it in a test tube with the nucleotides needed for the assembly of a new strand of DNA. This time they added the refined enzyme.

Very quickly a new strand of DNA was formed. Would it behave like natural DNA? The scientists separated the new strand from the natural strand on which it had been assembled. Then the separated artificial strand entered a bacterial cell, just as the natural strand would have done.

In about 20 minutes it had directed the invaded cell to manufacture several hundred duplicates of itself—the invading virus. When the new viruses broke out of the invaded cell they also were capable of infecting new cells. In this way scientists proved that DNA that had descended from an artificial parent could not be distinguished from the natural DNA.

At last it has become possible for scientists to produce genetic material in the test tube. In the future it may also be possible for scientists to alter the forms of DNA produced in the laboratory. Possibly a modified form of DNA might be delivered to a cell to replace a bit of DNA producing some dread disease in man and animals, such as certain kinds of cancer. Heart disease may be diminished when doctors learn how to control the creation of adrenal hormones, a particular protein that can over-excite the heart muscle. It may be possible to remake genes controlling the production of the hormone insulin and thus cure diabetes, a disease that occurs when the body does not receive its quota of this hormone.

As scientists continue to probe the mysteries of DNA, RNA and the cell as a whole, benefits to the field of medicine—and to the sick—will increase accordingly. It is conceivable that one day far, far in the future we will not only cure or prevent ailments of all kinds, but we will also control the evolution of all living things on earth.

Relief for Hemophiliacs

This boy wears braces to keep a crippling amount of blood from collecting in his joints. He suffers from hemophilia, the "bleeding disease," which is caused by a defective gene. In the future, these genes may be repaired by doses of chemicals to speed production of blood-clotting protein.

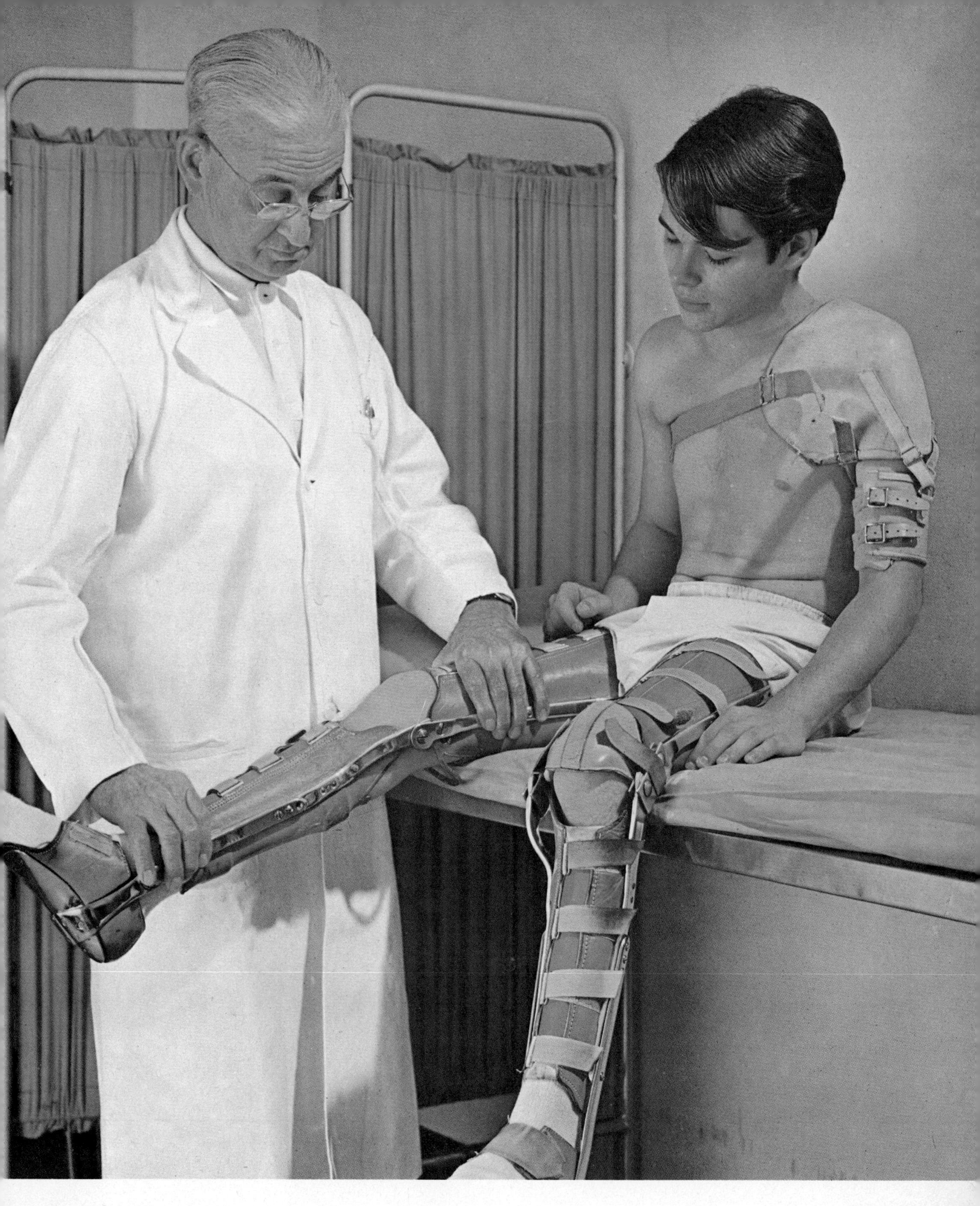

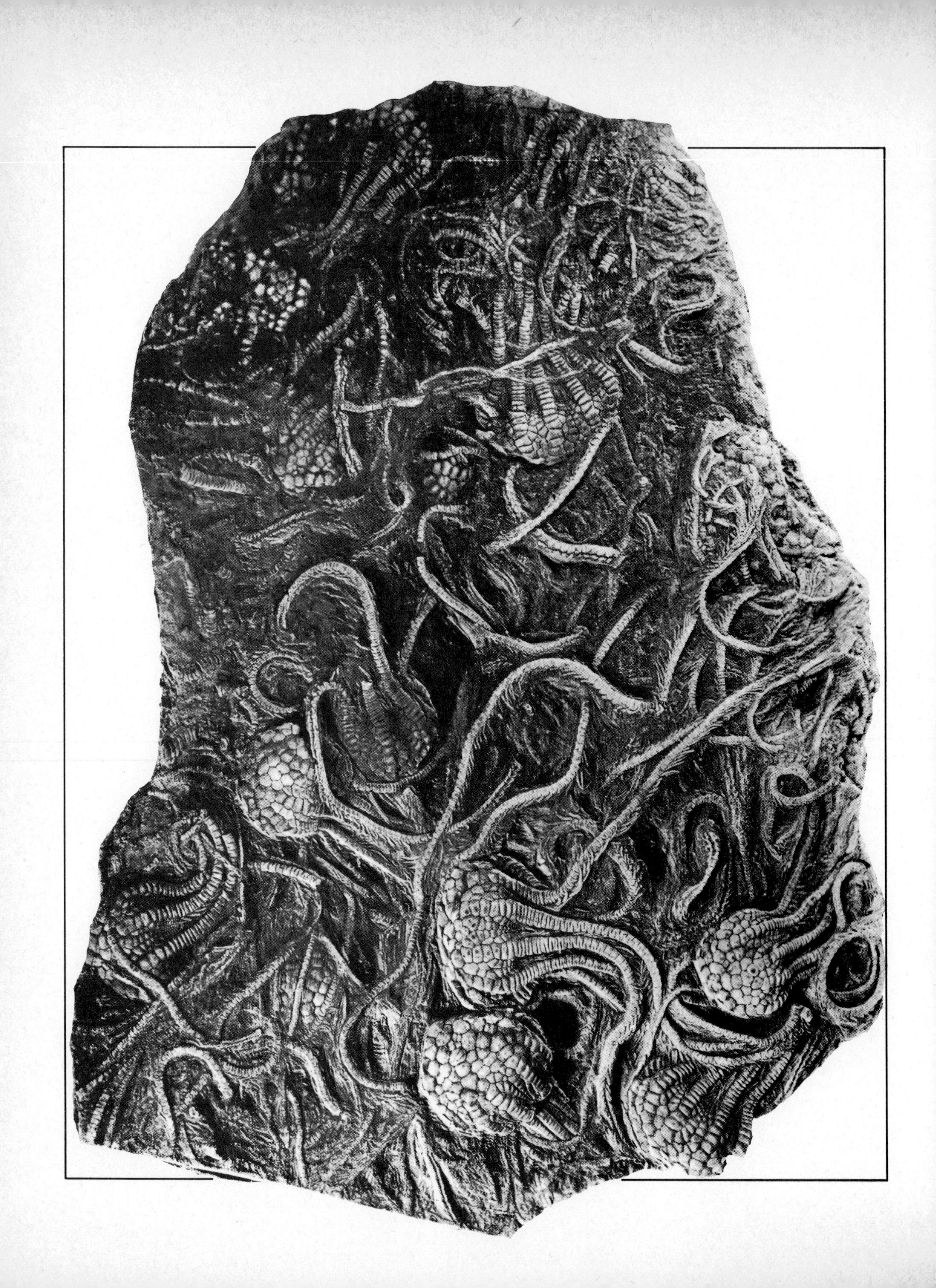

5

A Half Billion Years of Creation

STONY SEA LILIES of the extinct species called *Uintacrinus socialis* were preserved in the crust of Kansas 90 million years ago. At that period a shallow ocean covered the plains, and these animals related to starfish drifted about on the surface, collecting food along hair-lined grooves in their long arms.

Long before Darwin scaled the high sea cliff in the Cape Verde Islands and found sea shells buried in its limestone face, men had been digging shells, petrified wood and other ancient objects from the earth. Some of these curios strangely resembled the bones of animals. A few authorities held that they had been molded into these shapes by Satan to trick mankind, but most believed that fossils had been formed by natural forces in chance imitation of life.

The Reverend John Ray, a 17th Century Cambridge University lecturer, was enough of a naturalist to realize that some of the fossils he collected in the mountains were exactly like shells he gathered on the seashore. Others were obviously the remains of fish that lived only in the ocean deeps. To explain why marine fossils were found in the mountains, Ray fell back on Old Testament history. He concluded that the fossils were washed up to these high places when the Bible's 40 days and 40 nights of steady rain filled the reservoirs of the world and caused the "Fountains of the Great Deep" to break forth. In the tremendous flood that flowed over the earth, he said, the fish and other

creatures of the sea were simply swept up rivers and carried through underground streams, right into the mountains.

The "flood theory" of fossils was finally destroyed by the knowledge that the face of the earth, with its mountains and valleys and plains, was slowly shaped by continuing natural forces like wind and water—as geologist Charles Lyell had said. But it took some doing, by the infant sciences of geology and archeology, to give this evolutionary idea enough time to operate in a few thousands of millions of years instead of a few thousand years. Not until the start of the 19th Century did the French scholar Lamarck make a convincing case for the theory that fossils were not the results of chance or devilish shapes of stone, but the natural remains of once-living plants and animals.

Paris nevertheless became quite excited when Lamarck's colleague, Georges Cuvier, professor of natural history at the Collège de France, announced in 1796 the discovery of

Layers of Ancient Life

Ribbon-striped cliffs like these in Australia are often a fossil treasure chest. Composed chiefly of limestone, the cliffs were once part of the ocean floor, where sediment collected, trapping sea creatures of the time. Then pressure from the accumulating matter turned the sediment to rock, sealing in the fossils. About a million years ago, this section rose above sea level—and revealed its ancient life.

elephant bones in the soil of the Paris area itself. Soon Cuvier and other diggers were unearthing even stranger members of an unknown past—reptiles as big as whales, mammoths with long tusks and heavy coats of hair, bears, wolves and other creatures that only vaguely resembled living species. From a few of their bones Cuvier put the animals back together with such startling realism that the writer Balzac marveled: "Is Cuvier not the greatest poet of our century? . . . He picks up a piece of gypsum and says to us 'See!' Suddenly stone turns into animals and another world unrolls before our eyes."

Like the living members of the animal kingdom, such collections of ancient animals could be classified into species and genera (groups made up of many species). Cuvier counted 90 species and some whole genera that had completely disappeared from the earth. What could have brought about such widespread extinction, and how could the lost species have been followed by still

(Text continued on page 87)

Tracing Plant Evolution

The seven key steps in the evolution of plants are shown on this chart. The line of progression, running from the bottom to the top, spans some two billion years. Except for the first oxygen-producing plants, of which little is known, a drawing of a representative fossil species illustrates each step. Because of gaps in the fossil record, no one is able to say with certainty how the seven groups are related to each other. But botanists who study fossils assume that as a new group branched out it produced at least one offshoot different and adaptable enough to make the next great advance. While a new group formed the old group became increasingly specialized.

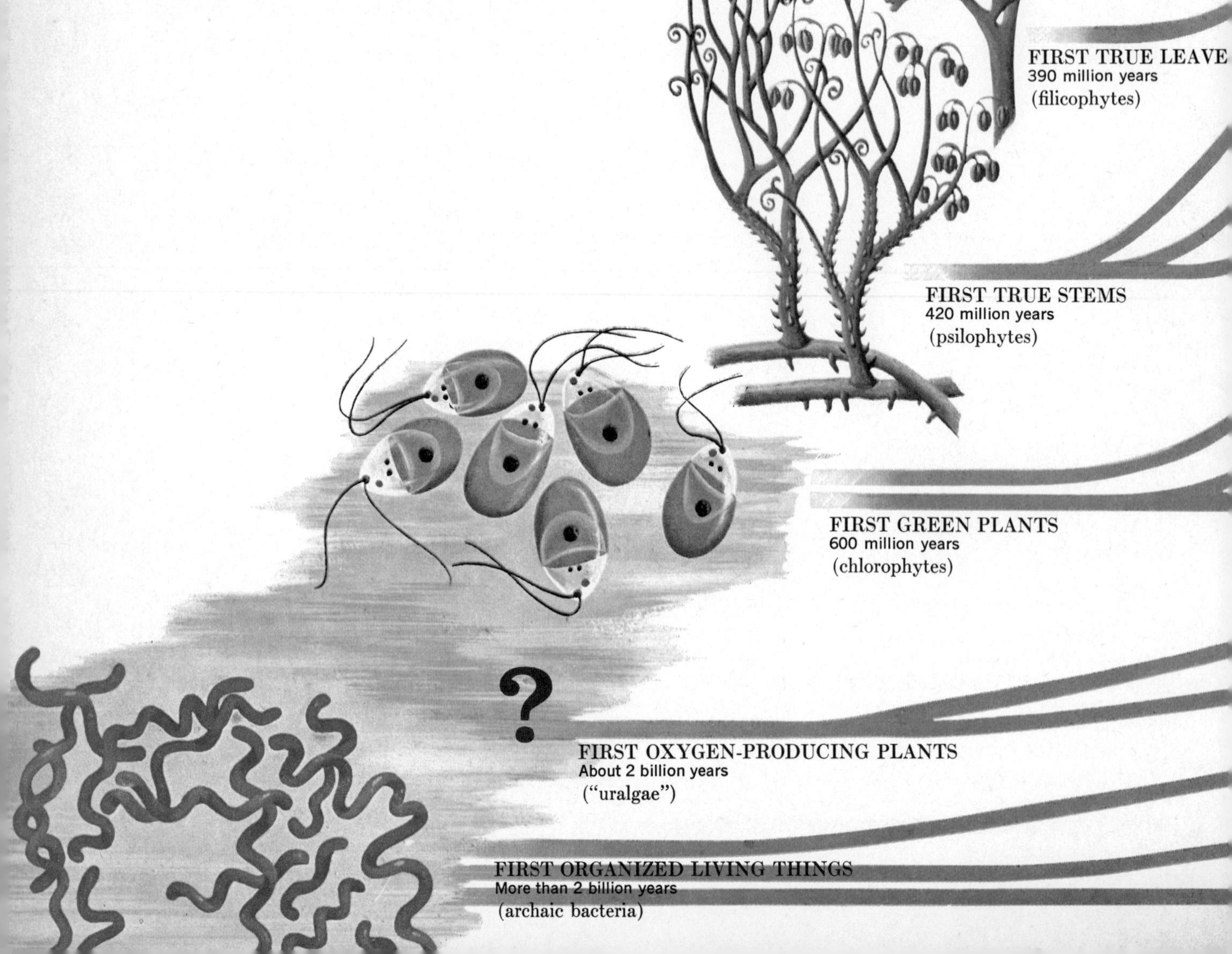

FIRST TRUE LEAVE
390 million years
(filicophytes)

FIRST TRUE STEMS
420 million years
(psilophytes)

FIRST GREEN PLANTS
600 million years
(chlorophytes)

?

FIRST OXYGEN-PRODUCING PLANTS
About 2 billion years
("uralgae")

FIRST ORGANIZED LIVING THINGS
More than 2 billion years
(archaic bacteria)

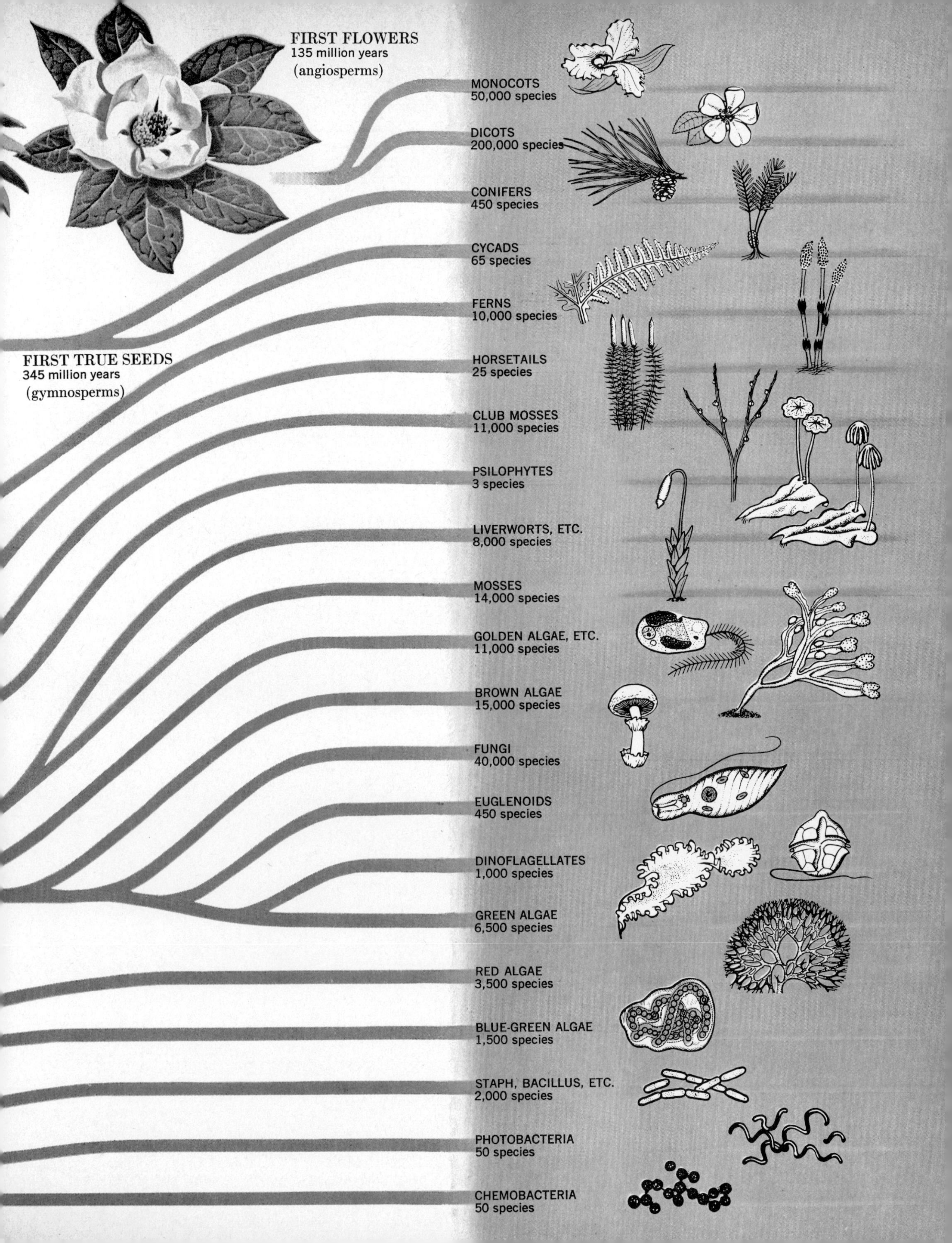
FIRST FLOWERS
135 million years
(angiosperms)
MONOCOTS
50,000 species
DICOTS
200,000 species
CONIFERS
450 species
CYCADS
65 species
FERNS
10,000 species
FIRST TRUE SEEDS
345 million years
(gymnosperms)
HORSETAILS
25 species
CLUB MOSSES
11,000 species
PSILOPHYTES
3 species
LIVERWORTS, ETC.
8,000 species
MOSSES
14,000 species
GOLDEN ALGAE, ETC.
11,000 species
BROWN ALGAE
15,000 species
FUNGI
40,000 species
EUGLENOIDS
450 species
DINOFLAGELLATES
1,000 species
GREEN ALGAE
6,500 species
RED ALGAE
3,500 species
BLUE-GREEN ALGAE
1,500 species
STAPH, BACILLUS, ETC.
2,000 species
PHOTOBACTERIA
50 species
CHEMOBACTERIA
50 species

Plants from the Past

The whisk fern *(above)* and the horsetails *(right)* closely resemble plants that existed around 400 million years ago. The leafless whisk fern, which has neither true leaves nor roots, is a direct descendant of some of the first plants to develop an internal plumbing system. The horsetails have no roots either, and their primitive "leaves" are not the green spikes—these are branches—but the dark marks on the stems.

others before the animals of today appeared?

To find the answers to such riddles, Cuvier set out to learn all he could about the fossils and the ancient earth in which they were buried. With Alexandre Brongniart, a professor of mineralogy, he studied the Paris countryside in depth. He discovered that layer was piled upon layer: one stony bed filled with millions of sea shells, and just below it, a different formation with a scattering of land shells. Other layers were studded with the bones of extinct giant mammals. Still others had no fossils at all.

Cuvier and Brongniart tried to interpret this puzzling series of vanished worlds. At times, they explained, the seas had flooded into the Paris lowland. At other times the salt waters had receded, and the dry land had been dotted with fresh-water lakes. Again the seas had returned, and again they had rolled back. In deposits laid down during the sea eras were the shells and bones of ocean life; in sediments marking the bottoms of the fresh-water lakes lay fresh-water shells and the bones of land animals. There was no mixing of the land and sea deposits; one ended and the other began.

This discovery was a most disturbing one. Cuvier was a scientist devoted to the truth, but he was also a religious one, and even with the succession of species before him he could not admit that one species had arisen from another. Cuvier preferred another explanation, that a series of vast upsets in the natural

(Text continued on page 90)

INSECT BEGINNINGS 300 MILLION YEARS AGO
More than 300 million years of insect evolution appear in the paintings on these two pages. Although there were probably some earlier insects, the first recognizable fossils date from the Upper Carboniferous period, whose trees were the source of modern coal. These insects included "dragonflies" with a 30-inch wingspread.

MEGANEURA

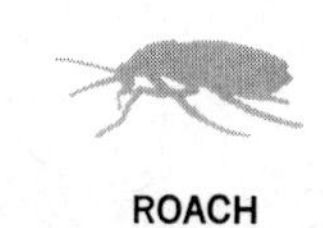

ROACH

STENODICTYA

THE APPEARANCE OF GRASSHOPPERS
The Permian period, 280 million years ago, saw the emergence of reptiles like the sailfinned *Edaphosaurus* *(left background)*. While these lumbering creatures ruled the land, insects were unchallenged in the air. Among the species was an early grasshopper, *Oedischia,* with slender antennae and strong jumping hind legs *(left foreground)*.

OEDISCHIA EARLY STONEFLY PROTOTELYTRON EARLY MAYFLY

AN ANCESTRAL CRICKET

Just about all the insects that existed in the Triassic period 230 million years ago are still alive today, an example of survival that no higher animal can equal. But the wing being gulped down by the lizard here was six inches long and belonged to one species that has not survived, a possible ancestor of the modern cricket.

EARLY SAWFLY

EARLY SILVERFISH

ANCIENT INSECTS THAT THRIVE TODAY

Dinosaurs like *Allosaurus* dominated the landscape and the flying reptile *Rhamphorhyncus* ruled the air in the Jurassic period 180 million years ago. However, insects thrived and most of the fossils found from this period are familiar forms—such as the earwig, and the dragonfly about to be devoured by the *Rhamphorhyncus*.

CADDISFLY

DRAGONFLY

EARWIG

DRAGONFLY

PLANT LOUSE

A KENYA MANTID

A PERUVIAN LEAF MANTID

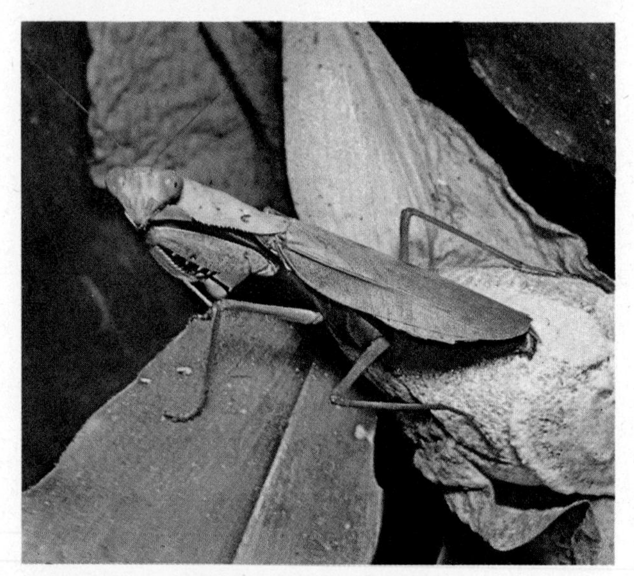

A MANTID FROM THE CONGO

A RHODESIAN MANTID

world wiped out the old and cleared the stage for new creations.

Darwin, faced with the same relationship, saw that living species were the modified descendants of fossil species. In *The Origin of Species* and in *The Descent of Man,* he decided that an unbroken chain of organisms had lived between the first forms of life and man. Here was a theory hopefully subject to proof; where was the proof? The fossils found up to Darwin's day were little help. Where were the missing links?

The search went on in Europe, in the Americas, in Java, in China, in Africa. By the middle of the 20th Century, a hundred years after publication of *The Origin of Species,* the fossil record was still far from complete, and it never would be complete. But it was filled in well enough that scientists could begin to trace the evolution of life in terms of its fossilized remains.

The record was now complete enough that a severe test could be made. Would the remains in the rocks show the spread of new gene arrangements, as the theory of evolution required? Could evolutionary change be

A MADAGASCAR LEAF-LITTER MANTID

A CONGOLESE LICHEN MANTID

tracked through one population after another of various species? There was some doubt that so difficult a task could be carried out. Nevertheless, such men as George Gaylord Simpson, E. H. Colbert, Theodosius Dobzhansky, A. S. Romer and Ernst Mayr proceeded to put together the complex story of the rise and development of life on earth.

The story is well documented through all but the opening chapters. Our planet and the rest of the solar system are now thought to be about 4.5 billions years of age, and for most of that time the earth was without life. In the very oldest exposed rocks, which have been dated as far back as 3.6 billion years, there is no trace of fossils, and for good reason. If life began as a molecule with the miraculous ability to reproduce itself, developed later as a single cell and then into a cluster of soft cells, it could not have left even the shadowiest trace behind. Yet somewhere on earth, somehow, life began, possibly more than two billion years ago. It was already old by the time its first traces—single-celled microorganisms, which were neither plant nor animal—were left in the rocks.

(Text continued on page 96)

Safety Through Disguise

By assuming amazing likenesses to their surroundings, plants and animals are often able to survive simply because they can escape detection by their enemies. In the pictures here, a number of insects called mantids match themselves with uncanny skill to the twigs and leaves on which they live in various parts of the world. Another ability helps make this protective mimicry work—mantids can hold absolutely still.

The Mighty Dinosaurs

The rulers of the Age of Reptiles were the dinosaurs, all of which belonged to two groups, saurischian and ornithischian. The former, represented in the color drawing by the towering *Tyrranosaurus rex (left foreground)* and the "ostrich dinosaurs" *(left background)* had small hip bones like those of more primitive reptile ancestors *(diagram above)*. The ornithiscians, represented by the creatures at far right, developed heavier hip bones *(diagram below)* adapted to the four-legged gait that some members of each group used.

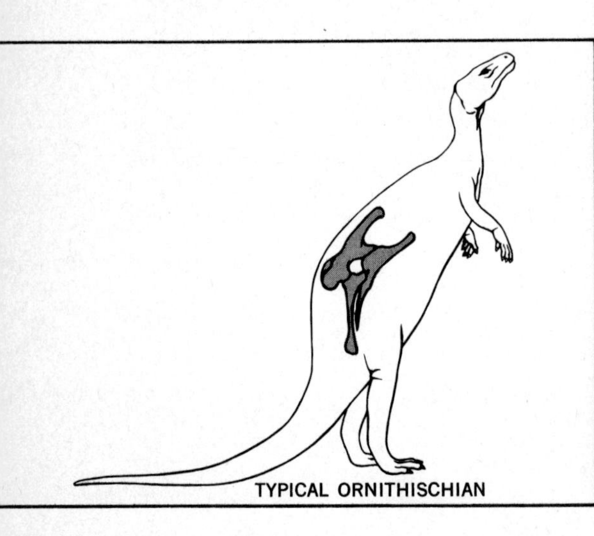

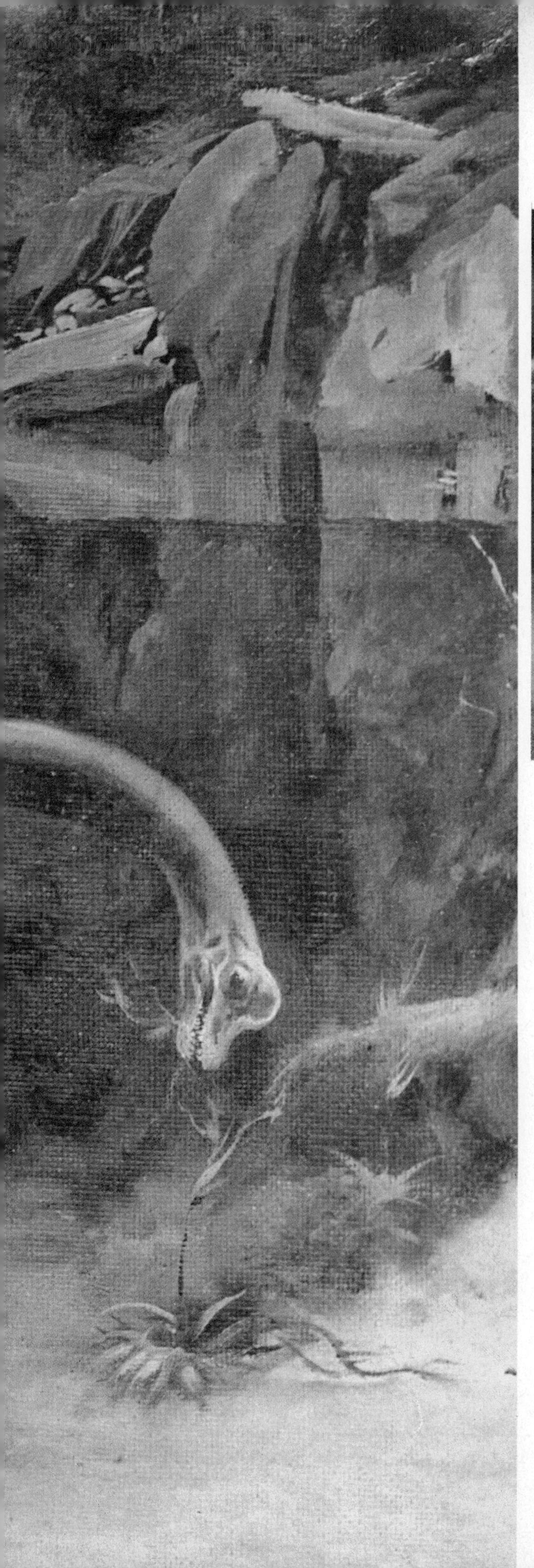

The Biggest Dinosaur of All

The swamp monster *Brachiosaurus* was a saurischian type of dinosaur that developed a four-legged gait despite its relatively light hip bones *(pages 92-93)*. In fact, it evolved into the largest animal of all time, except for the modern whale, and measured up to 80 feet long and 40 feet high. The *Brachiosaurus* was apparently so heavy that its bones would have been crushed if the body were not at least partially supported by water.

The earliest animal fossils so far found are those of primitive water-dwelling invertebrates—animals without backbones. Already they were quite advanced in structure. Some had jointed bodies and shells. They were in fact creatures well adapted to their environment, the ancient, silent seas. Then, in rocks formed about 425 million years ago, the remains of a new kind of creature appear. Named an ostracoderm and looking like a crudely formed fish, it had a skeleton, and it was armored with bony scales. But it still had no jaw, and made its way along the bottom, sucking up food.

As time went on, this creature began to lose out to something still newer in the world, a fish with jaws. Some of the jawless fish, it appears, were born with a slightly different gill arch that was shaped like a V turned sideways: with only a few related changes the V made a jaw. A fish so equipped no longer had to scavenge along the bottom; it could hunt many kinds of food at any level.

The bony jaw, like any favorable change, spread throughout the fish population. Then these early jawed fishes, the placoderms and acanthodians, were themselves replaced by different and still more successful descendants. Mutation and selection produced better fins for better swimming. The new fishes had tail fins, which with a gentle back-and-forth motion could drive them forward. Other fins served as stabilizers and controllers of movement. Fishes so equipped went on to occupy all of the earth's waters and finally outnumbered all other vertebrates combined.

But a fish that differed significantly from all the earlier ones appeared in the rocks laid down about 390 million years ago. The front of its skull could be raised and lowered a bit, a change that would ease the shock when the jaws snapped shut. Its teeth were sharply pointed and well adapted to grasping prey. A single bone connected the fins with the middle part of the skeleton. Such a single bone and related structures were to become familiar in later ages as the leg bones of land-dwelling animals. These unusual fish, called crossopterygians had made an even more vital change. In addition to gills, they were developing lungs, and as such were distant but direct ancestors of man.

Some 365 million years ago, some of these crossopterygians ventured out on the land. They probably lived in streams that dried up in summer into scattered pools. Did the fish struggle and flop from one drying pool to another with more water? No one knows, but those fish that were able to stay out of the water for a longer time certainly would have been the survivors—and would have left behind descendants even better equipped to breathe in the air.

In eastern Greenland, fossil hunters have found a creature more advanced than the most advanced crossopterygians: a primitive amphibian. The *Ichthyostega* combined a fish tail with lungs and well-developed legs and feet. With their lungs and "walking legs," these early fish-out-of-water had a whole new source of food open to them. They could crawl along the banks of streams and snap up the insects that were beginning to swarm there. The earth lay open before them—for no other vertebrates were around.

During the next 50 million to 100 million years, the early amphibians spread far and evolved into many different species. Their fossilized bones and imprints are found in Europe, North America and parts of Asia. These newcomers to the land, however, never succeeded in wholly freeing themselves from the past. They could rely on their lungs and they had legs, but they always returned to the water to lay their eggs.

After a long time, mutation and selection again performed their wonders. Some of the amphibians developed an egg that was covered by a firm, leathery shell and thus was far better protected than the soft eggs of the fish and the other amphibians. This new and better egg was deposited in some safe place on land until the young were hatched. With its perfection, the egg-laying animals won their full freedom from the water. Inside the egg, a well-protected embryo could develop in its own private "pool," guarded not only from dryness but also from the hazards of the world outside. The new and freer group that was evolving in this way, from amphibian ancestry, was the reptiles.

The oldest fossil eggs ever found come from sediments in Texas dated at about 280 million years ago. When the eggs were laid the reptiles were already well advanced. It is therefore difficult for scientists to tell exactly where the dividing line is between amphibians and reptiles.

With their new-found freedom from the water, the reptiles literally took over the earth, and the "age of reptiles" began. For the first time, the land was widely occupied by vertebrate life. As time went on, the reptiles split into a great many groups with different structures and different ways of life. Some of the reptiles returned to the water and continued to breathe with their lungs. Their legs gradually evolved into paddles or fins. Some of these marine reptiles looked strikingly like modern whales and porpoises.

Still other reptiles ventured into the air. With wings formed by a fold of skin, functioning like those of the modern bat, these reptiles hunted from the sky, swooping down to seize fish that swam near the surfaces of lakes and lagoons.

Yet for all their ability to fly, these reptiles did not give rise to the birds. Fossils prove that the birds arose independently, from the same ancestors—the archosaurs—that produced the flying reptiles. Two of the earliest birds fell into a coral lagoon in what is now Bavaria, in Germany. As the fine lime ooze settled around them, they were preserved in remarkable detail. The long head with its sharp teeth, the long neck, the strong hind legs and the rich, herringbone pattern of feathers all are molded in the most exquisite detail on the fine limestone. If the long flight feathers and the unique row of feathers down either side of the tail had not been imprinted

HOT PERIOD: EARLY CROCODILES

TEMPERATE PERIOD: TAPIRLIKE ANIMALS

in stone, few would agree that so reptilian a creature could have been so clothed. But the feathers were true bird feathers and the fossil, named *Archaeopteryx,* is classified as a bird, the earliest and most primitive of the group that in time would take over the province of the air.

When the reptiles were in their first heyday, one of their small groups began to change. Some of the animals skulking through the lush swamps had longer and slimmer leg bones than those of other reptiles. Their improved ability to get around counted heavily in natural selection. These were the synapsids, which were to form an evolutionary bridge between the reptiles and what would become the mammals. Reptilian life was spreading out in all directions at the time and synapsids, like other subclasses, came in a variety of shapes and sizes—everything from wolf-sized creatures to brutes of half a ton or more. One order among them, the therapsids, was a curious mixture of reptile and mammal. Unlike most reptiles, the therapsid had a secondary palate, enabling it to breathe while eating. Instead of the simple peg teeth of the reptiles, it had sharply contrasted incisors, canines and cheek teeth—for chewing food instead of bolting it whole. Its legs were drawn underneath its body, a useful height above the ground. This new, higher-slung animal was much faster when the need arose than the typical reptile, which had ungainly legs and a body that tended to drag along the ground.

Among the descendants of the synapsids were some small, warm-blooded animals with

Animals and Climate

These drawings show how animal life in one place, Germany, changed with changes of climate. In the humid Jurassic period 170 million years ago, the Mystriosaurus, an early crocodile, lived in warm lagoons *(far left)*. By the Eocene, 50 million years ago, the climate had grown cooler and drier, and animals resembling tapirs *(left)* had appeared. Some time in the last million years, during the extreme cold of the Pleistocene period, woolly mammoths *(right)* were common and roamed throughout western Europe.

COLD PERIOD: WOOLLY MAMMOTHS

uniform body temperatures. A coat of hair helped to protect them from the heat as well as the cold. Perhaps at first there were very few of them, for not many of their bones have been found. The few fragments do not show positively how they produced their young. Although they may have been egg-layers like their reptilian ancestors, they may also have suckled their young.

From the standpoint of natural selection, suckling of the young turned out to be all-important, one of the great changes of all evolutionary time. The fish and reptiles laid large numbers of eggs, but relatively few of them ever hatched, and not many of the untended young survived. But the small animals nursing their young suddenly made the survival of offspring less a matter of chance than of fitness to survive.

The new mammals, for that is what they were, had only a few offspring. But the food supply of these few was assured and they were protected as no other creatures' young had been. Thus the few, in the end, could outnumber and outlast the many. At about the same time, perhaps 100 million years ago, selection developed another great improvement—the placenta, an arrangement of blood vessels through which an embryo could be supplied with food and oxygen while developing inside the mother's body. With this protection at a critical stage, the mammals' future was set.

After the reptiles began to decline, the mammals branched out phenomenally and began to move into every part of the earth. During the next 27 million years there

(Text continued on page 103)

The Mixed-Up Platypus

This odd creature, called a platypus, is found only in Australia and Tasmania. Although it is a mammal, parts of its body are reptilian, other parts birdlike.

A

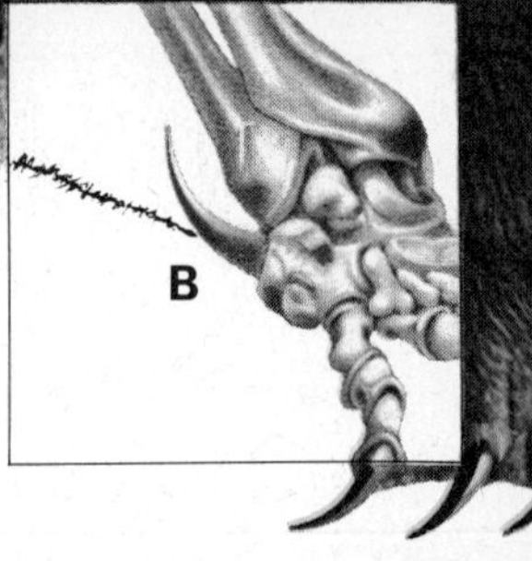

THE FLAT, MUSCULAR TAIL (A) is much like a beaver's, except that it is covered with fur instead of scales. The tail stabilizes the platypus when it swims, and helps in dives.

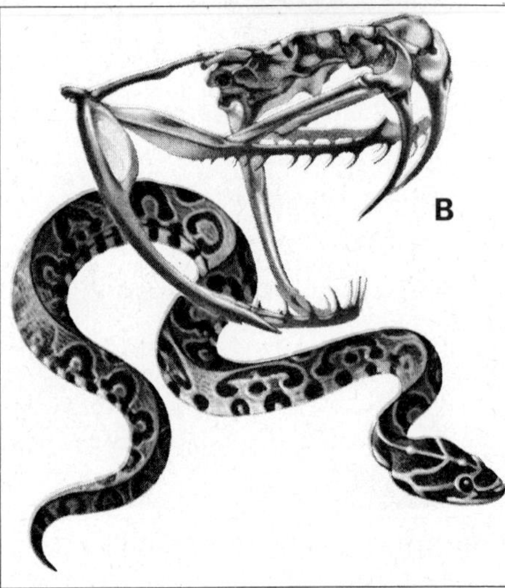

THE CURVED POISON SPUR (B) on a male's hind leg is similar to the fangs of a poisonous snake. Like the fangs, the spur carries venom, though a less deadly type.

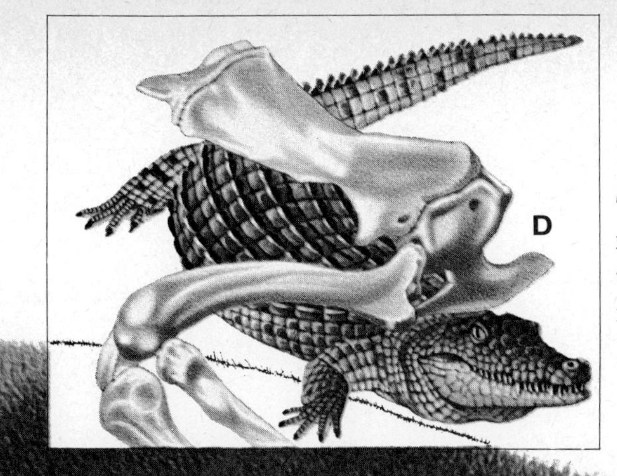

THE SHOULDER BONES (D) recall a remote reptilian past. This connection of the forelimbs is clumsy, and the platypus must shuffle along close to the ground.

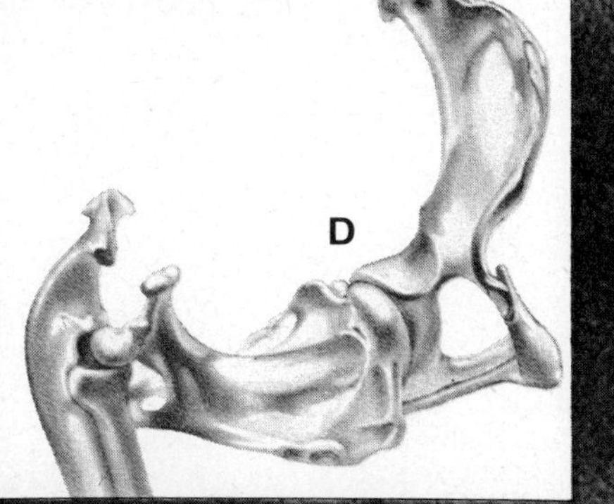

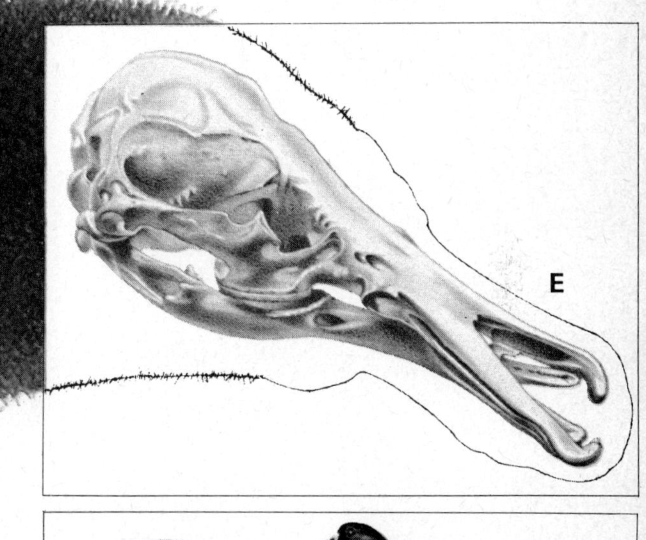

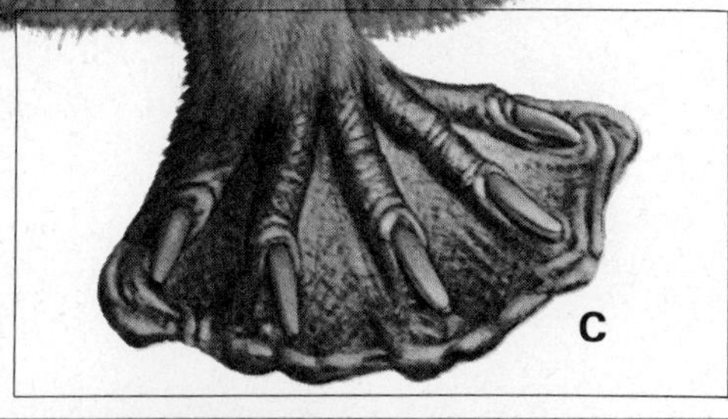

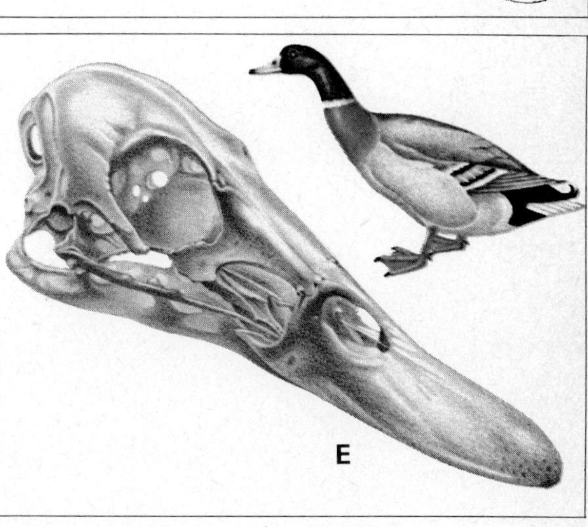

THE WEBBED FOREFOOT (C) is like the otter's, except that its skin extends past the toes to make an extra-large paddle. On land, the webbing folds back for the claws to dig.

THE DUCKLIKE BILL (E) helps the platypus seek food on mud bottoms, as a duck does. The platypus bill, however, is sensitive, unlike the duck's horny bill.

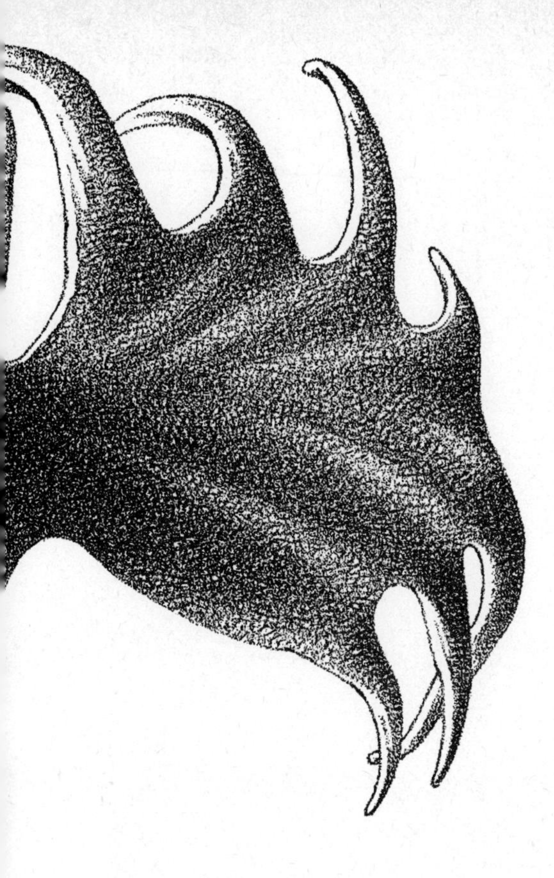

Extinct for Reasons Unknown

No one knows for sure why the Irish elk became extinct, but we do know that it disappeared during the Pleistocene epoch, which some geologists say extends back to two million years ago. Its tremendous antlers, which may have served as an advantage at one time, perhaps later prevented the animal from moving rapidly enough to escape new kinds of predators such as early man.

evolved every mammalian order now existing—and many that have become extinct.

Among this great assortment that spread over the earth were the tree shrews and some of their relatives. They were of vast importance: they apparently founded the primate family, whose branches led to the monkeys, the apes and man. Not much larger than squirrels, the tree shrews had slightly bigger brains than those of their ancestors. Their fingers and toes had a greater range of movement, which helped as they climbed high in the trees in search of insects and fruit.

Some of the tree shrews' relatives developed a hand that could close quickly and surely around a branch, and slender legs that let them hop nimbly through the trees. These were the lemurs, which once lived in many parts of the world but flourish today mainly on the island of Madagascar, off the east coast of Africa. The lorises, now living in India, Southeast Asia and Africa, developed forward-turned eyes, which all higher primates have. Another relative was the tarsier, which had a more efficient grasp and was generally adapted for life in the trees. By about 25 million years ago some early primates like this had evolved into monkeys, a variety of apelike animals.

The green world of the treetops in which the primates lived was a safe but restricted one. A strong sense of smell and acute hearing were not as essential as on the ground. The primates with freer hands and better eyes were the ones to survive such hunters as snakes and such hazards as falling to the ground—and to leave descendants. Gradually the primate brain changed from a primitive "smell" organ to a more advanced "sight" brain. Along with enlargement of the brain came a rounding out of the head and, in some of the African primates, enlargement of the whole body. This forced some groups to develop a different way of moving about. Too heavy to run through the branches, holding fast with hands and feet, they took to swinging along with a new motion of the arms, called brachiation.

One of these arm-swinging, apelike creatures, called *Proconsul,* lived about 20 million years ago. Some of his descendants are the great apes of today—the gorilla, the orangutan, the gibbon and the chimpanzee. Another apelike creature, called *Ramapithecus,* lived at roughly the same time as *Proconsul,* but his descendants seem to have developed quite differently. In time they adopted a more varied diet and came down from the trees to look for food on the ground. Slowly they changed along a line quite different from that of the other apes—a line that led to man.

The Hunter and the Hunted

A Tengmalim's owl swoops down on a rodent in a forest, continuing the ancient struggle for survival today, much as it always has been carried on. If all forest rodents were as easy to spot and catch as the one here, deaths would outnumber births more and more until the rodents became extinct.

6
The Search for Mankind's Ancestors

A BABOON'S SKULL stares sightlessly from limestone rock between two wedges that will pry it loose. Scientists believe that the fossil head of this baboon—one of a species now extinct—was crushed by a crude stone weapon perhaps wielded by a predecessor of man.

People used to have strange ideas of early manlike creatures. Even men of science thought they might have had human heads, foot-long tails and bodies as shaggy as a bear's. Others simply said that man had no early predecessor, that he was created as he is today.

Both versions of man's origins suffered a rude upset in 1856. In the little Neander Valley near Düsseldorf, Germany, an extraordinary skull fragment and some limb bones were discovered in a limestone cave. The skullcap was thick, with huge ridges over the eyes. In studying the skull, the scientist Thomas Huxley found that the cranium, where the brain had been, could hold as much water as the cranium of a living primitive tribesman. He also decided that the limb bones were "quite those of an European of middle stature. . . ." Neanderthal man, Huxley concluded, was a human, and not an intermediate between apes and man.

Who were this early man's ancestors? The question fascinated a young Dutch doctor, Eugène Dubois, who reasoned that any form between ape and man would probably have originated either in Africa, where the gorilla and chimpanzee still exist, or in Malaya, where the orangutan survives. Dubois was able to persuade the Dutch government to send him to Java, in the Malayan region, where he began to explore an area in the center of the island.

Four years after he had set out from The Netherlands, Dubois brushed earth away from the fossil he had crossed half the world to find: a thick, chocolate-brown skull. It was apelike but different from any ever seen before. Dubois was not sure of what he had found until he dug out a long bone nearby. As a doctor, he knew what it was: a thigh bone like that of a human, belonging to a being that had walked upright. Dubois named this creature *Pithecanthropus erectus:* from *pithekos,* the Greek word for "ape," and *anthropus* for "man."

To those unwilling to believe that man was linked to apish ancestors, *Pithecanthropus* was an insult, and many people criticized Dubois harshly. In 1895, disheartened and hurt, he locked the fossils in a strongbox in the Teyler Museum in Haarlem, his hometown, and permitted no one to see them for the next 28 years.

While the bones of Java man were locked away, a young Canadian physician and biologist, Dr. Davidson Black, accepted an appointment as professor of anatomy at Peking Union Medical College in China, because he thought that man might well have originated in Asia. One day Dr. J. G. Andersson, a Swedish geologist, walked into Black's office with two teeth found on a hillside at Choukoutien, near Peking. For centuries the Chinese had been mining "dragon bones" there. When pulverized they made a prized medicine.

As Black examined the teeth from this hill, his hopes soared. He was certain that they came from a very ancient human. At Black's urging, the Rockefeller Foundation agreed to finance a full-scale scientific exploration of

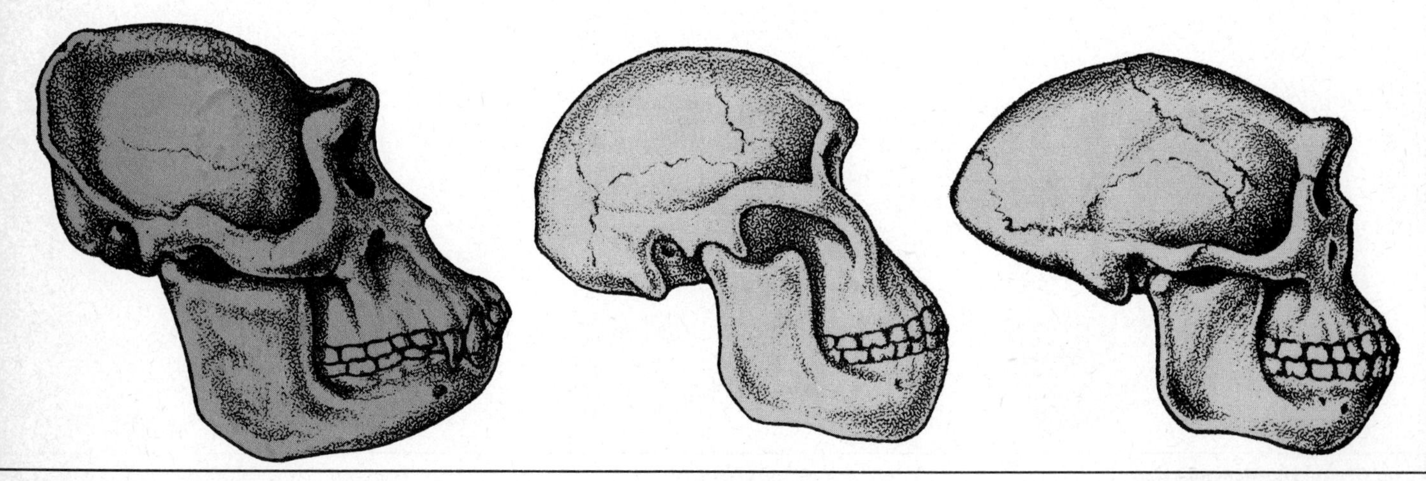

SIMIAN AUSTRALOPITHECUS PITHECANTHROPUS IV

Choukoutien. Here, in 1927, the first scientific expedition in the search for man's origins began its spadework.

Three days before the first season's work was to end, Dr. Birgir Bohlin, the field supervisor, found another early human tooth. Black studied the new tooth night after night. It differed so much from all the others in his large collection of plaster casts that he decided upon a bold step. He set up a new genus and species for the man from whom it came: *Sinanthropus pekinensis* (Chinese man of Peking).

After two years of work, Dr. W. C. Pei, an associate of Dr. Black, found the object of all their searching—a nearly complete skullcap. It was partly surrounded by loose sand and partly embedded in rock. At first glance, Pei felt certain that it was a skullcap of *Sinanthropus* and rushed it to Black. A few nights later Black showed it to Roy Chapman Andrews, the American scientist. "There it was . . ." Andrews wrote, ". . . one of the most

The Evolution of Man's Skull

As modern man evolved from his apelike ancestors, the shape and structure of his skull developed in a fairly regular pattern. Man's early ancestors *(far left)* had thick, heavy skulls with large jaws and small brain spaces. But as later creatures moved up the evolutionary ladder toward modern man, their skulls became progressively higher, their jaws became lighter and smaller and the spaces occupied by their brains grew larger.

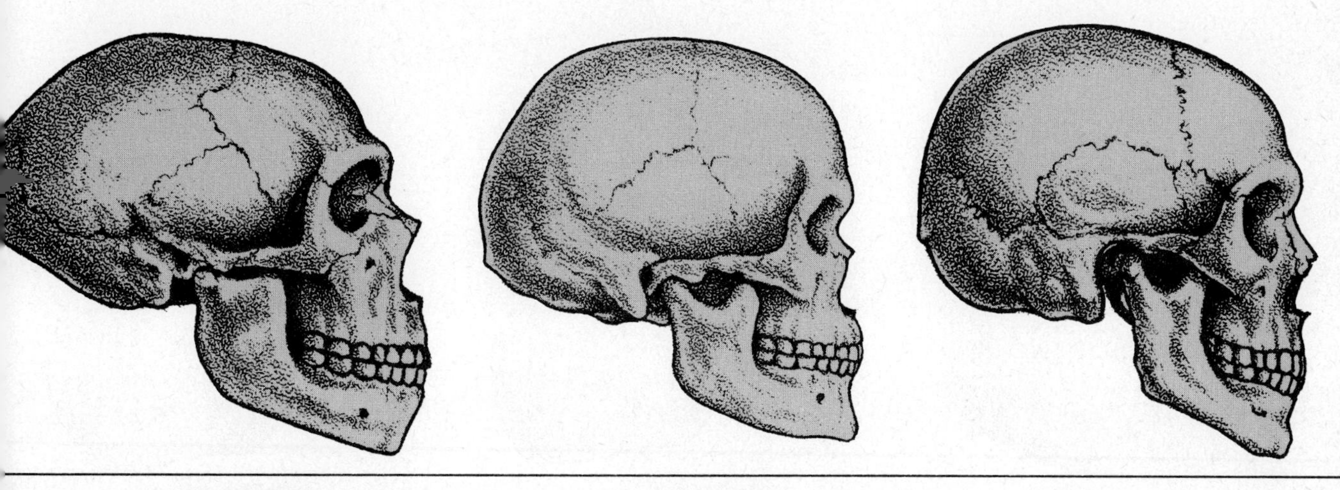

NEANDERTHAL CRO-MAGNON MODERN

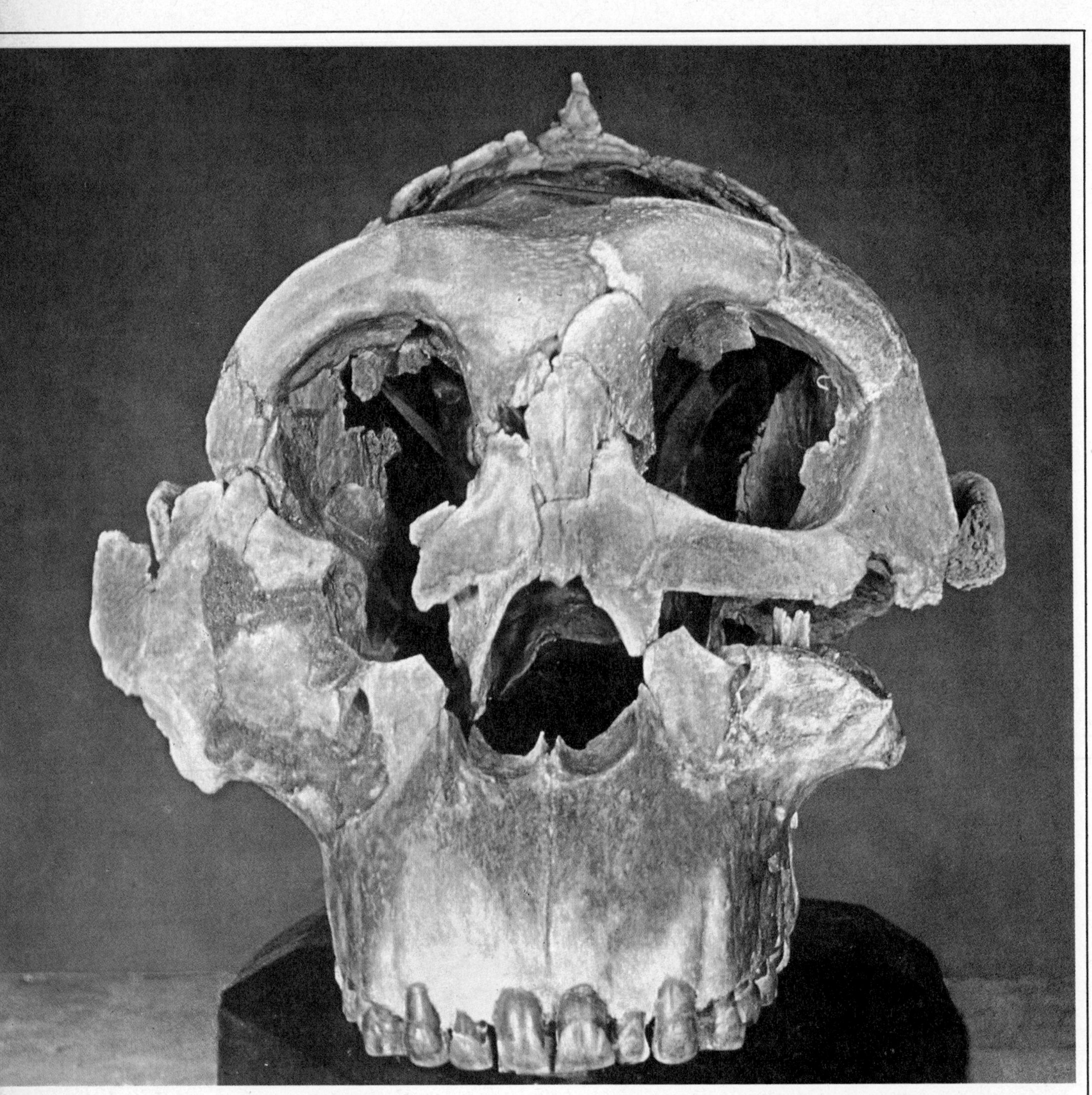

A Face from the Past

Found in the Olduvai Gorge in Tanzania, the skull above belonged to *Australopithecus boisei.* These creatures eventually died out, but their close relatives, *Australopithecus africanus*, are thought to have evolved into primitive man.

important discoveries in the whole history of human evolution."

The discovery made headlines around the world. The work at the hill was reorganized on a broader basis, and in the 1930s the pieces of a second *Sinanthropus* skull came to light. Black died suddenly in Peking in 1934, but the Rockefeller Foundation found a successor in Dr. Franz Weidenreich, a German professor of anatomy at the University of Chicago. Weidenreich had already completed world-famous studies of evolutionary changes in the pelvis and foot, changes that made possible man's upright posture. His studies underlined the belief of Darwin and Huxley that man is a descendant of some ancient anthropoid stock.

In China, Weidenreich began a classic series of studies of Peking man that supported the conclusion of Black: *Sinanthropus* was indeed a human, though a very primitive one. What placed him solidly in the human race was his undoubted ability to walk upright on two legs.

The teeth and dental arch of *Sinanthropus* were also manlike. The canine teeth were not the projecting fangs of an ape; they did not come together like the blades of a pair of scissors. And the dental arch was curved, not oblong in shape.

Still another proof lay in the skull. Weidenreich arranged the skulls of a gorilla, a Peking man and a modern man in a row. Even a glance revealed their striking differences: the skull of the gorilla was flat in shape, the skull of Peking man was somewhat higher and the skull of modern man was nearly round. The low skull of the gorilla could house a brain of about 450 cubic centimeters; the higher dome of Peking man, one of about 1,000 cubic centimeters; and the high cranium of modern man, a brain of about 1,350 cubic centimeters.

However, Weidenreich pointed out that cultural objects such as tools, rather than the size of a brain, are the only true guide to intelligence. At Choukoutien, many such objects were found. The continuing excavations produced thousands of chipped-stone tools. They were simple, with only a few chips removed, but they were made to a pattern. Some of them were found with charred bits of wood and bone that lay on hard-baked red and yellow clay. These were hearths: Peking man had mastered the use of fire.

Soon after the big excavations began in China, the Geological Survey of The Netherlands East Indies invited a young German paleontologist, G. H. R. von Koenigswald, to resume the search for early man in Java. Von Koenigswald found the skull of another *Pithecanthropus* almost exactly like the first. After examining Java man and Peking man, von Koenigswald and Weidenreich agreed that they differed little more than "two different races of present mankind." In recent years, these intriguing creatures, along with others like them from Africa, have been assigned to an extinct species, *erectus*, of our own genus *Homo*. This means that they like the Neanderthals, were defi-

The Evolution of Stone Age Tools

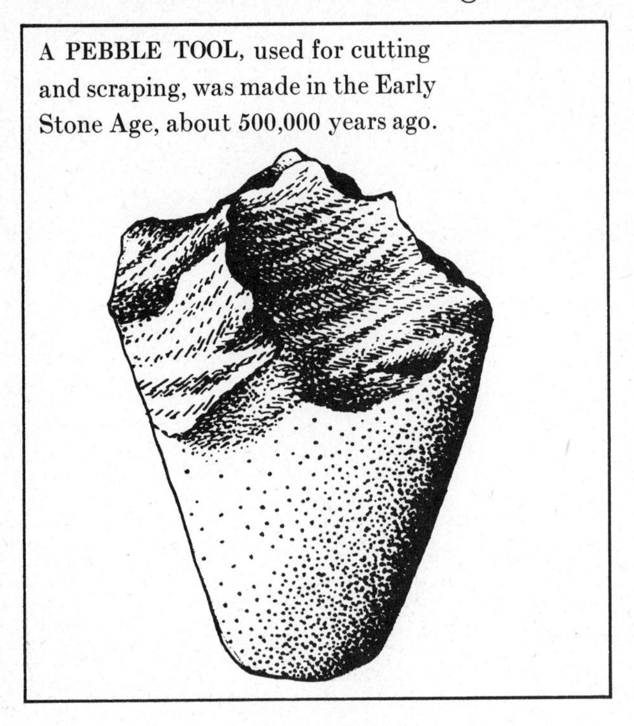

A PEBBLE TOOL, used for cutting and scraping, was made in the Early Stone Age, about 500,000 years ago.

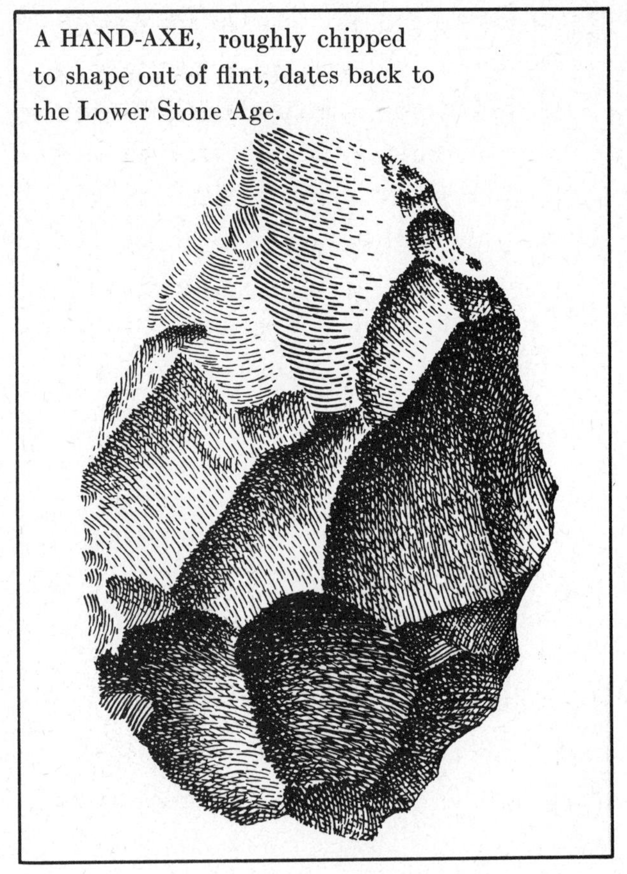

A HAND-AXE, roughly chipped to shape out of flint, dates back to the Lower Stone Age.

nitely human—not part ape and part man.

Where, then, was a manlike ape, a real "missing link?" Actually, there were several around by this time but the scientific world had not yet accepted them. Dr. Raymond A. Dart, a professor of anatomy in South Africa, had discovered the first of the missing links in 1924 in the form of a child's skull. This skull, found near Taung, in South Africa, seemed to belong to an ape with human features. There was no beetlelike brow but a true forehead. The upper jaw, instead of jutting forward as in all true apes, was shortened and set back under the skull. The permanent molars were just beginning to come in, and the canine teeth as in humans were quite small. The set of the skull and the opening for the spinal column suggested that this child had walked upright. No ape can take more than a few steps without going down on all fours.

Dart lay awake nights "in a fever of thoughts" about what kind of ape might have lived long ago in this semidesert plateau of South Africa. For millions of years—while ice had advanced and retreated over much of the earth and while mountains rose along the continental coasts—South Africa had stood as a dry, relatively undisturbed veld, much as it is today. The nearest natural habitat of apes was more than 2,000 miles away from Taung. Could some different kind of ape have found a way to adapt itself to conditions of life in an arid, open land?

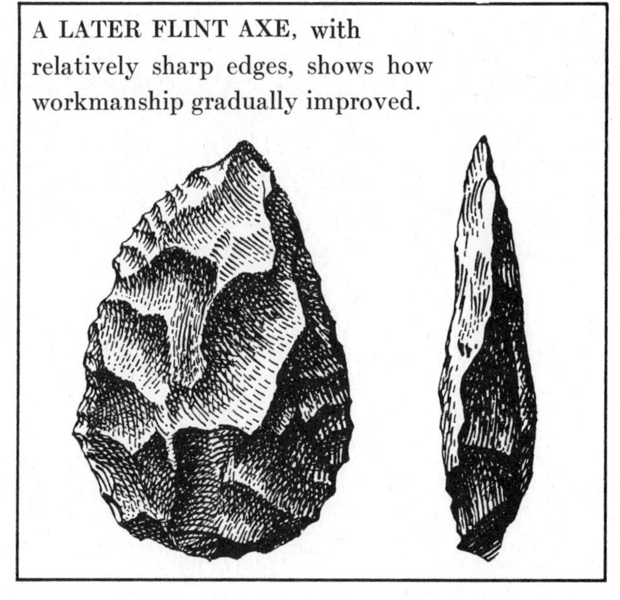

A LATER FLINT AXE, with relatively sharp edges, shows how workmanship gradually improved.

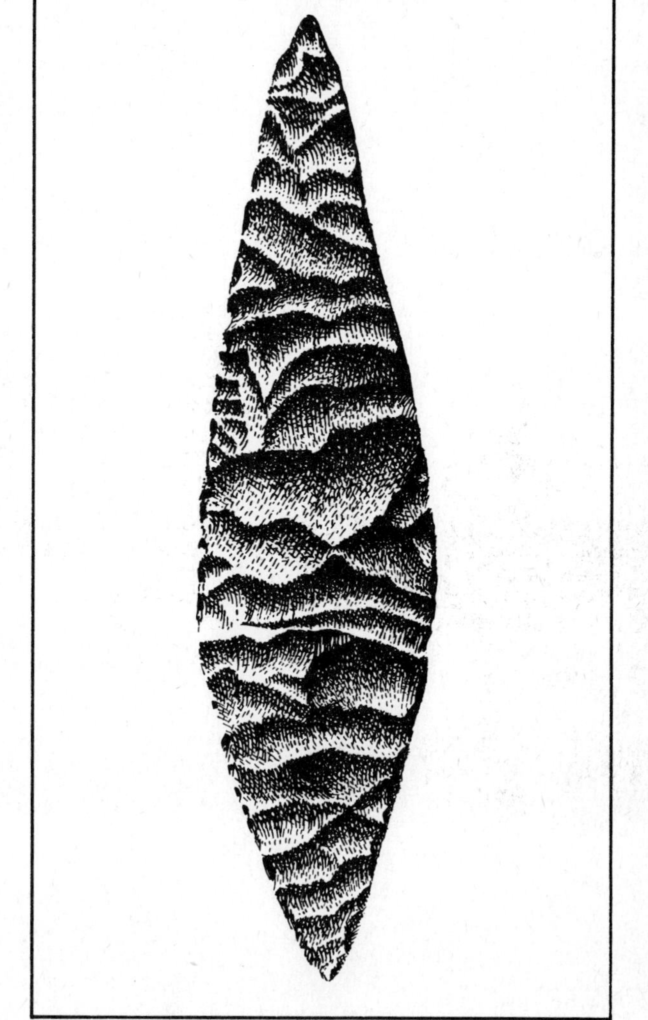

A PRESSURE FLAKED DAGGER was produced some 5,000 years ago, at the beginning of the Bronze Age.

Boldly, Dr. Dart set up a new genus for his ape-child: *Australopithecus africanus—Austral* for "south." Criticism from the scientific world was not long in coming, but Dart was encouraged by a warm letter of congratulation from Dr. Robert Broom, a Scottish physician who had hunted fossils all over the world. Two weeks later, Broom appeared at Dart's laboratory in person. He too was convinced that as "a connecting link between the higher apes and one of the lowest human types," the Taung baby was the most important find made up to that time.

Some years later, Dr. Broom found another *Australopithecus* at Sterkfontein, a fossil-rich area near Pretoria. On Broom's second visit to Sterkfontein in 1936, G. W. Barlow, manager of the local quarry, handed him something he thought might interest the scientist. Indeed it did. Barlow had given him two-thirds of a "beautiful fossil brain cast" which had only that morning been blasted out of the rock. The next day Broom not only recovered the base of the skull and both sides of the upper jaw, but also fragments of the brain case. When the fragments were pieced together, Broom had most of the skull of an adult *Australopithecus.*

Australopithecus Africanus

The ape-man at left, called *Australopithecus africanus,* ran upright on two legs, and probably used his hands to throw rocks and wield weapons. Believed to be modern man's oldest known predecessor, he lived in South Africa some two million years ago.

Three years after this find, Barlow handed Broom another discovery—an ape-man's upper jaw with one molar in place. Barlow had obtained it from a schoolboy, Gert Terblanche, who lived on a farm at Kromdraai, less than a mile away.

The doctor drove over to Kromdraai, and during the next two days he and the boy found a number of scraps of bone and teeth as they sifted the earth. When the pieces were put together, Broom had most of another ape-man skull, the third. The face was flatter than the Sterkfontein *Australopithecus,* the jaw heavier and the teeth larger, though more human in shape.

Kromdraai man differed so markedly from both the Taung child and the Sterkfontein adult that Broom set up a new genus for him: *Paranthropus robustus* ("robust near-man"). Scientists now believe that this man is a different species of the same genus that the other two belong to, and have reclassified him as *Australopithecus robustus.*

During World War II further digging was impossible, but soon after the war Broom resumed work at Sterkfontein. By 1949 the remains of more than 30 individuals had been recovered from the South African caves, and Le Gros Clark at Oxford undertook a careful, detailed study of them. His verdict was that in some respects the *Australopithecus* fossils were definitely apelike creatures, with small brains and large jaws. Yet they differed from

Peking Man

More than 300 thousand years ago, Peking Man, a member of the extinct species *Homo erectus,* left his remains in a cave in Northern China. There he lighted fires, killed deer, made stone tools and probably used language. His broken bones—apparently split open deliberately—indicate that he and his fellows practiced cannibalism.

recent or fossil apes, and at the same time they were close to the family of man.

They also made tools, which Dr. Weidenreich had pointed out are essential in establishing human status. The tools, made of stone, were first found in 1953 in South Africa's Vaal Valley, which had been formed in the same period in which the ape men lived.

Later, nearly 300 tools were located at Sterkfontein. To the untrained eye they would have looked like naturally broken stone. But close examination showed that chips had been deliberately flaked off two sides of each stone; the head of the stone was left round. Such a hammer stone, held in a hand and guided by the intelligence that had shaped it, could cut, scrape and probably kill.

Although the discovery of even such primitive tools was greeted with intense interest, other stone tools had been found many years earlier in East Africa by Dr. Louis S. B. Leakey, an archeologist. He had first come upon the tools in 1931 on an expedition to Tanzania's Olduvai Gorge, an abrupt break in the earth some 25 miles long and 300 feet deep. The expedition took seven days to cover the 500 miles from Nairobi to the gorge, a wild place often visited by lions. One visit was enough to convince Leakey that Olduvai was a site "such as no other in the world." Stone tools were so plentiful at the bottom of the gorge and in its lowest layers that Leakey

(Text continued on page 119)

Swanscombe Man

Wielding wooden spears, Swanscombe hunters close in for the kill. Swanscombe man, who hunted along the brooks of the English countryside more than 200,000 years ago, had thicker bones than modern man, but no other essential differences so far as is known. The tusk sinking into the sand at the center of this painting belonged to an elephant like those seen parading past on the riverbank in the distance. The skull in the foreground belonged to a huge Ice-Age ox.

Neanderthal Man

A Neanderthal father tries on one deerskin cape while his wife dresses another and their children roughhouse in the painting at left. A rugged early human breed, the Neanderthals roamed Europe and the Middle East about 40,000 to 75,000 years ago.

named their type Oldowan, after the place of discovery.

Leakey wondered if the tools could have been made by a creature similar to the one that Dr. Dart had found near Taung. If so, he was unable to find this creature, even though he had returned to the gorge again and again with his wife and their two sons, over a period of 28 years. It began to look as though the most primitive men had lived in one place, South Africa, and that the most primitive stone tools had been made in another, East Africa.

But on July 17, 1959, a bit of bone lodged in a rockslide caught Mary Leakey's eye as she crept along the hillside. She recognized it as a piece of skull. She searched higher along the slope, and suddenly saw two big teeth, brown-black and shiny, barely sticking out of the ground. They were twice as wide as the molars of modern man, but human in shape. The Leakeys went to work with camel's hair brushes and dentists' picks. The palate to which the teeth were fixed came into view, then fragments of the skull appeared. At the end of 19 days they had about 400 fragments.

While the delicate task of assembling the bits and pieces went on, the Leakeys continued to excavate the site. They not only discovered the oldest skull of a near-man found in all eastern and central Africa up to that time (1,750,000 years old), but they also found one of his campsites. Lying about were the fossil bones of animals—rats, mice, frogs, lizards, birds, snakes, tortoises, some young pigs and parts of antelopes. Nearly all these bones were broken, but the near-human skull and one human leg bone discovered at the same site were not. So this early man must have been the one who killed the animals for food.

As they pieced together this creature's skull, the Leakeys found it was that of a nearly mature male. In many ways the young male resembled the larger ape men of the *Australopithecus* family. But the face was not as ape-like as those of the South African fossils; the cheek had almost the curve of the human cheek. The palate was deeper and arched like that of modern man. The molars Mrs. Leakey had found were unusually large and heavy. Nevertheless, close study showed that they were like human teeth. Because of these differences, Leakey set up a new genus for his find, naming him *Zinjanthropus boisei* (*zinj* denoting eastern Africa in Arabic, *boisei* honoring Charles Boise, who had helped to finance the search).

"Zinj" has now been classified as a new species (*boisei*) of the genus *Australopithecus* first recognized in South Africa, and is no longer thought to have made the earliest tools that the Leakeys had first found in the 1930s. At present, scientists believe that these tools were produced by another hominid, or human type, one of which the Leakeys discovered two years after they found "Zinj." This man, perhaps a descendant of *Australopithecus africanus,* is considered to be the first member of our own genus *Homo*. He has been classified as *Homo habilis*.

A million years or so ago, some of these near-men of South Africa became globe-trotters. Wide continental ice sheets had crept down from the north, and as vast quantities of water were locked up in the deep ice, the sea level dropped. All through the world the shores widened, and land bridges were revealed, wide and crossable, between some of the earth's major land masses.

So early man pushed on to North Africa, Europe, India, Java and China. The provable record of man's evolution is still obscure through the middle Pleistocene epoch (500,000 to 150,000 years ago). But dating from the late Pleistocene, or glacial, period, a group of men distinctly different from all the more primitive types gradually became predominant in Europe and western Asia. These were the Neanderthals, whose brains, lodged in massive heads, were in the size range of modern human brains.

There are so many fossil remains of Neanderthal man that they have led to confusion instead of clarity; there are almost as many theories of his history, movements and mysterious fate as there are skulls or scholars. It is generally thought that there was at first a single racial group spread throughout Europe, but that the coming of the last ice age may have isolated the peoples of southwestern and southeastern Europe from those of eastern Europe and the Middle East.

Thus shut off, the western Neanderthals became very distinctive and developed even heavier eyebrow ridges and more massive jaws than they originally had. Conditions were different for the Neanderthals in eastern Europe and the Middle East. There the glaciers lay far to the north or were limited to the mountains. The wide plains and high plateaus supported large herds of animals, and roots and berries grew in the valleys. Bands of men could move about freely, and there was nothing to hinder different groups from intermixing.

Some of these eastern Neanderthals lived in hillside caves looking out on the Mediterranean, others in the caves bordering the fertile land of the Tigris and Euphrates Rivers. In many ways they resembled the early Neanderthals of Europe; they had sloping foreheads and massive, bulging brows. But remains in some Middle Eastern caves reveal a curious combination of Neanderthal and modern features. Those from Palestine most nearly resembled modern human skeletons.

In the caves the remains of *Homo sapiens,* or modern man, nearly always lie just above those of Neanderthal man, who simply vanished about 35,000 years ago. Although there is almost no mixing of Neanderthal and *Homo sapiens* remains, a few small fragments of bone have cast some doubt on this neat separation and suggest that the first of the modern men may have appeared in Europe 250,000 years ago, even before the Neanderthals held sway.

A nearly complete skull was found at Steinheim, Germany, in 1933. It would have held

Cro-Magnon Man

Three Cro-Magnon warriors, laden with game, return to their camp *(above)* after the hunt. Successors to Neanderthal men, the Cro-Magnons hunted in Europe during the late ice ages and recorded their feats in many cave paintings. They were large men who wore sewn clothes and used a wide variety of weapons.

a brain within the range of a modern brain and it had the characteristics of both Neanderthal man and *Homo sapiens.* Two years later some skull fragments and bones were found deep in very old gravels on the banks of the Thames River at Swanscombe, not far from London. The bones from Swanscombe look like those of modern man, a fact that impresses many authorities. If Swanscombe man lived at the time that gravels were laid down by the river, he would be about 250,000 years old; and if he is indeed a modern man, then his kind, *Homo sapiens,* is far older than anyone had thought.

The question is not settled. There is no doubt, however, that a modern form of man —*Homo sapiens* like ourselves—replaced Neanderthal man about 35,000 years ago. One area where this occurred is the beautiful Dordogne region of southwestern France. Here the green valleys are walled in by gentle limestone cliffs, many of them honeycombed with caves. Many of these caves were longtime homes of Neanderthal man.

Sometime after the Neanderthals disappeared, modern *Homo sapiens* moved in. These newcomers were Cro-Magnon man, named for the cave near the little village of Les Eyzies where their traces were first discovered. Though their brains were no larger than those of Neanderthal men, the Cro-Magnons put them to new uses. For one thing, they made a wide variety of improved tools and weapons.

The Cro-Magnons also became the earliest known artists. In some of the cave passages running back into the cliffs, these men, who were mighty hunters, began to scratch the outlines of the animals they pursued: mam-

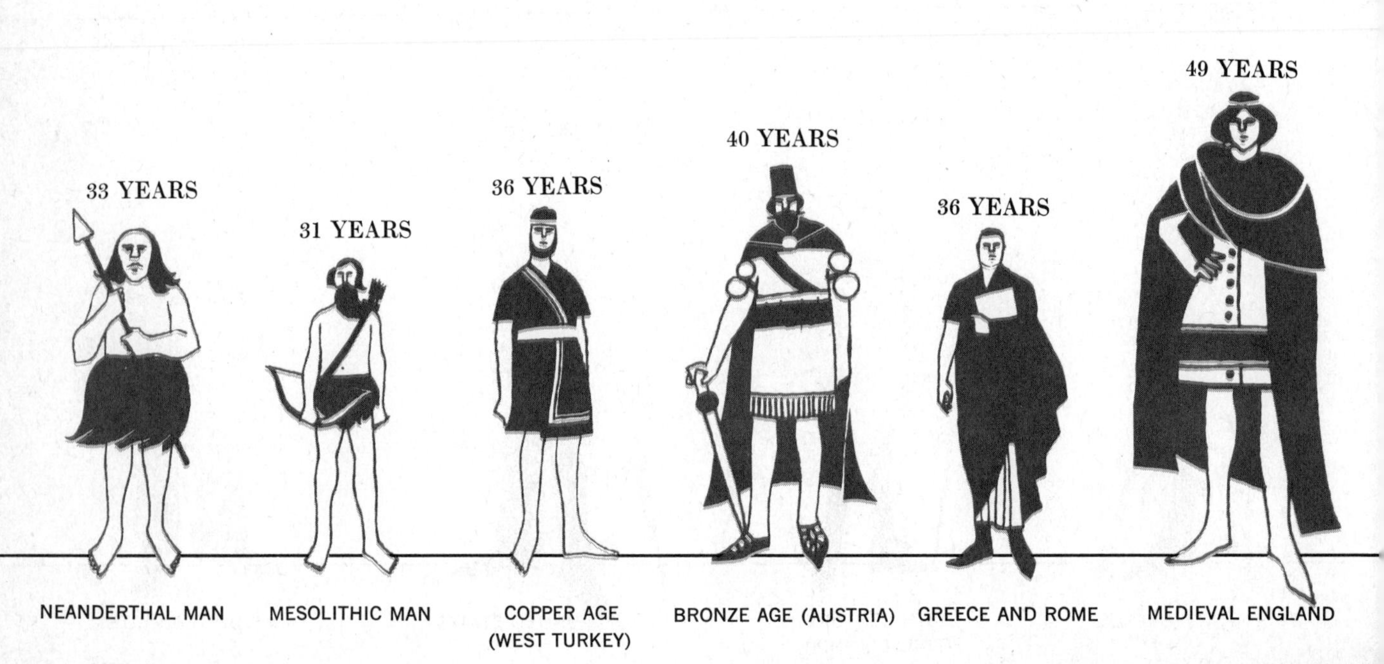

moths, horses, bison, wild oxen and rhinoceroses, as well as their favorite, reindeer. Soon they were outlining the animals in black on the stone walls of the caves, and in time they began to paint in colors.

By their art these new men of the caves proved they had come a long, long way: many of their caves were used only as places of ritual worship, and they supported some of their fellows as full-time artists.

No one knows for sure where Cro-Magnons came from. They may have arisen in one place and spread over the globe. Or according to another theory, several subspecies in different parts of the world may have progressed independently to *Homo sapiens* status, and gone on to develop into the present races of man. Whatever their birthplace or places, the new men absorbed or extinguished all others who had come before them.

The Advance of Life Expectancy

Today the average American can confidently expect to reach 70, but as the drawings below show, it has taken centuries for life expectancy to reach that point. Scientists believe that man's potential lifespan has always been the same—about 100 years—but until recent times, disease cut most men down before nature aged them. Note that in the cities of Ancient Greece and Rome and in such cities as Philadelphia in the 18th Century, life expectancy dropped, probably because of the outbreak of epidemics, often caused by squalid living conditions.

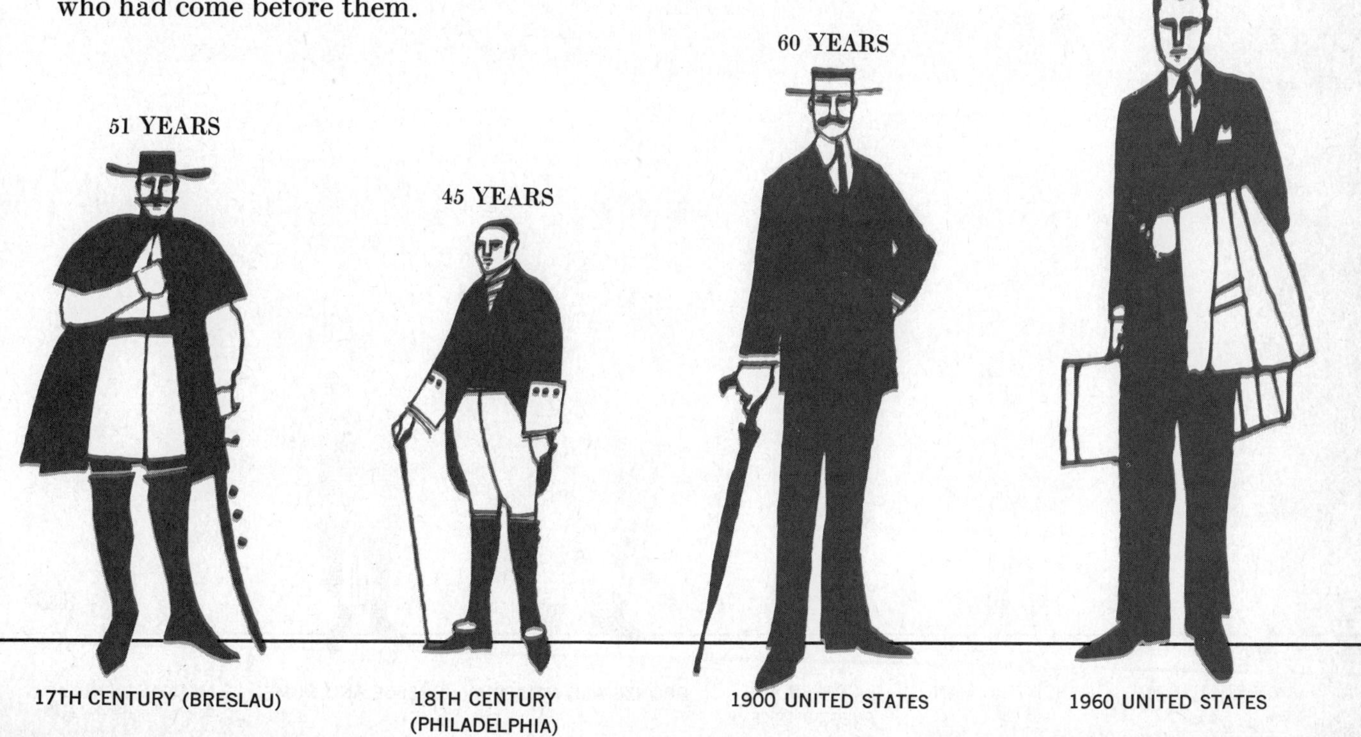

Even at the time of their earliest known appearance, these men who were inheriting the earth were biologically as advanced as any who have been born since. In brain size, in posture and in other physical ways the human beings who are alive today have not basically changed the pattern that evolution had already built into Cro-Magnon man. But what has won modern man his present control over the earth has not been his physique but his discovery and exploitation of a new kind of evolution. He began adapting the environment to fit himself. And he handed on to his descendants the information and traditions of his culture.

In adapting life to suit his own needs, man not only reshaped existing environments; he also invented new environments. He brought warmth and cold under his control and, to a great extent, flood and drought. By learning more efficient methods of producing and distributing food, he offset the danger of starvation. By harnessing energy sources greater than his own muscle power, he freed his species from limitations of time and space. And while the whole civilizing process introduced many new dangers, it wiped out or drastically reduced many old ones.

Something around two billion years has seen the evolution of life to date. Some four million years have seen the evolution of ape-man into the genus *Homo*. A single century has brought an understanding of the evolutionary forces shaping life. A few decades have unearthed the fossils and tools to demonstrate the actual events in the evolution of man, and of life in general. And even fewer years have revealed the base of it all, the miracle molecules of DNA. Only today is man realizing that as he reshapes his world and replaces physical evolution with a new, cultural evolution, he has the power for the first time to direct his future.

Herman J. Muller of fruit-fly fame, one of the most prominent genetic scientists in the world today, views this future with optimism. "Even as our own culture could not mean very much to the most superior ape," he states, "the culture of a mere million years from now will be so rich and advanced . . . that in it we, with our genetic constitution of today, would be like imbeciles in the palace. And so I believe that not only our cultural, but also our biological evolution will go on now to undreamed-of heights."

Five Basic Racial Types

All of the world's three billion human beings are descended from one or more of the five basic racial types of mankind *(right)*. The differences between one type and another have evolved slowly over years of natural selection, at least partly in response to differences in environment.

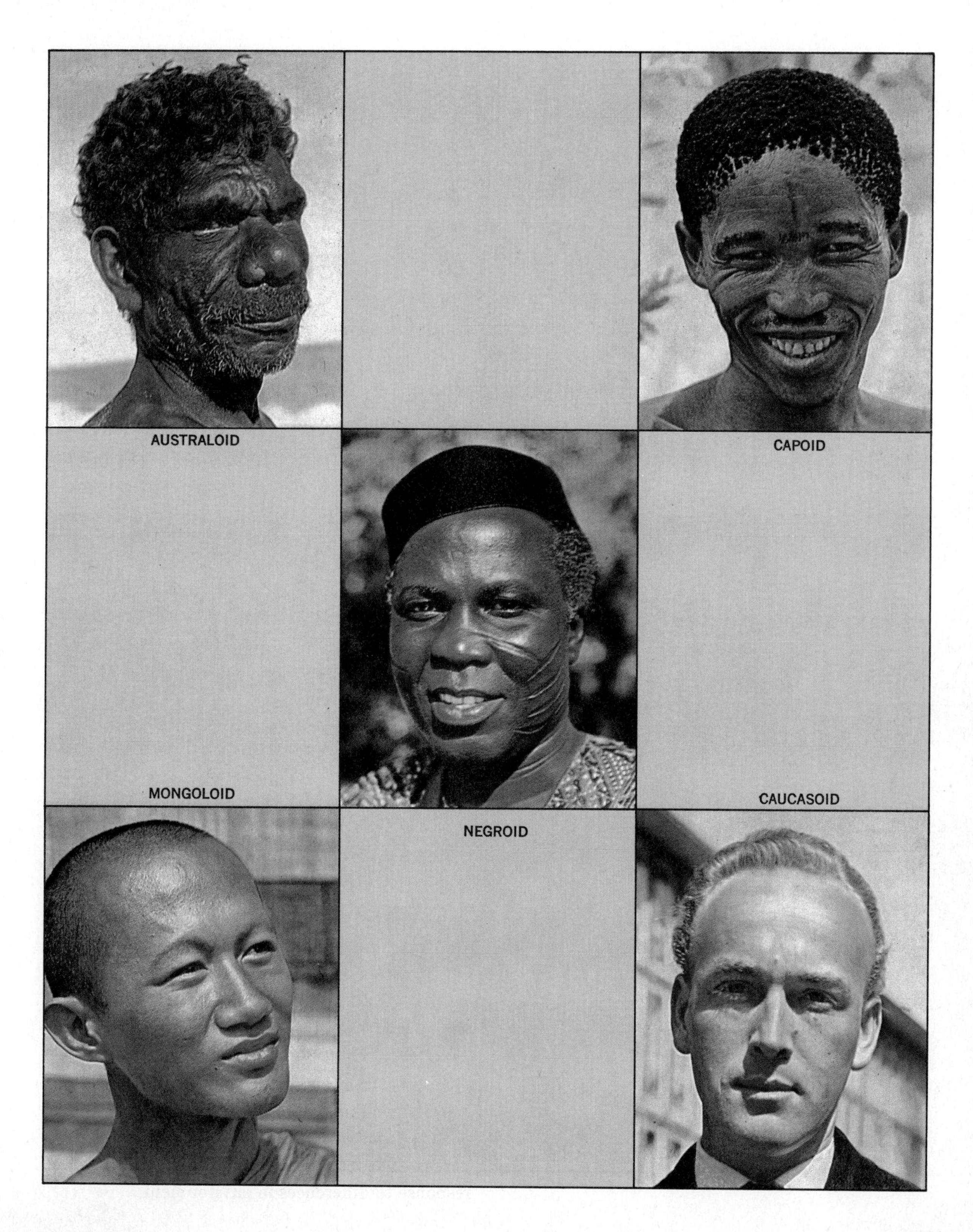
AUSTRALOID
CAPOID
MONGOLOID
NEGROID
CAUCASOID

Index

Numerals in italics indicate a photograph or painting of the subject listed.

Credits

The sources for the illustrations that appear in this book are shown below. Credits for the pictures from left to right are separated by commas, from top to bottom by dashes.

Cover—Mark Kauffman
Contents—Bob Kuhn—Guy Tudor—Matt Greene—adapted by Leslie Martin courtesy Clemens E. Benda: *The Child with Mongolism*, New York, Grune and Stratton 1960—Rudolf Freund—Allen Mardon
6—Culver Pictures
8—Bob Kuhn
10,11—Adolph E. Brotman, Colonel Charles Wellington Furlong
12,13—Adolph E. Brotman—Dr. Robert I. Bowman
14-15—Jean Zallinger
16,17—Rudolf Freund, Dr. Robert I. Bowman
18-19—John Markhan
20-21—Jack J. Kunz
22-23—Rolf Blomberg
24—W. H. Hodge courtesy Wards Natural Science Establishment, Inc.
27—Enid Kotchnig based on a drawing in *Principles of Insect Morphology* by R. E. Snodgrass, McCraw-Hill Book Co., Inc. 1935.
29—Lowell Hess
30,31—Dr. Alexander B. Klots (2), Dmitri Kessel, Dr. Alexander B. Klots
32—Drawings by René Martin from photographs by, Dr. H.B.D. Kettlewell
34,35—Lilo Hess
36,37—W. Suschitzky, Guy Tudor
38,39—W. H. Hodge except left centre and left bottom —George Kalmbacher
40,41—Dr. Alexander B. Klots, Rudolf Freund
43—Jürg Klages from Black Star
44—Jack J. Kunz
46-47—Henry H. Jones, drawings by Jack J. Kunz
48—drawings by Matt Greene, Brown Brothers
49—Matt Greene
50-51—Antonio Petruccelli
52,53—Thomas D. McAvoy, Eric Schaal, John Zimmermann, Larry Burrows, Thomas D. McAvoy, Robert W. Kelley
54-55—Kenneth Gossner
56—Rudolf Freund
58-59—Peter Stackpole
60—Courtesy National Archives
62-63—Gaetano Di Palma
65-68 Fritz Goro
70-71—Otto van Eersel
73—Fritz Goro
74,75—Robert W. Kelley, Herbert Gehr
76—Patricia Byrne
77—Adapted by Leslie Martin courtesy Clemens E. Benda: *The Child with Mongolism*, New York, Grune and Stratton, 1960
79—Fritz Goro
80—Mildred Adams Fenton
82-83—J. N. Jennings
84-85—Matt Greene
86-87—Walter Dawn, Charles R. Wyttenbach
88-89—Antonio Petruccelli
90-91—Dr. E. S. Ross from California Academy of Science
92-93—left top and bottom, Stephen Rogers Peck, right from *Prehistoric Animals* by Professor J. Augusta and Z. Burian, Paul Hamlyn Ltd.
94-95—from *Prehistoric Animals* by Professor J. Augusta and Z. Burian, Paul Hamlyn Limited
98-103—Rudolf Freund
104-105—Jan Lindblad from Photo Researchers, Inc.
106—Dr. John T. Robinson, University of Wisconsin
108-109—Helen Speiden
110—Des Bartlett
112,113—Matt Greene
114-118—Maurice Wilson for B.B.C. School Publications courtesy the Natural History Museum, London, copied by Derek Bayes
121—Maurice Wilson for B.B.C. School Publications courtesy the Natural History Museum, London, copied by Derek Bayes
122-123—Allen Mardon
125—left Jane Goodall—Camera Press from Pix, centre Eliot Elisofon, right Marshall Expedition Peabody Museum of Harvard University—Smithsonian Institution—Thomas D. McAvoy
End papers—Gloria Cernosia du Bouchet

For Further Reading

Adler, Irving and Ruth Adler, *Evolution*. John Day Co., 1965
Adler, Irving, *How Life Began*. John Day Co., 1957
Ames, Gerald and Rose Wyler, *First Days of the World*. Harper and Row, 1958
Andrews, Roy Chapman, *All About Dinosaurs*. Random House, 1953
All About Strange Beasts of the Past. Random House, 1956
Colbert, Edwin H., *Millions of Years Ago: Prehistoric Life in North America*. Thomas Y. Crowell, 1958
Darling, Lois, *Before and After Dinosaurs*. William Morrow, 1959
Darwin, Charles, *The Voyage of The Beagle:* abridged and edited by Millicent Selsam. Harper and Row, 1959
Dickinson, Alice, *The First Book of Prehistoric Animals*. F. Watts, 1954
Dudley, Ruth H., *Partners in Nature*. Funk and Wagnalls Co., 1965
Edel, May, *The Story of Our Ancestors*. Little, Brown and Co., 1955
Fenton, Carroll Lane, *Life Long Ago: The Story of Fossils*. John Day Co., 1964
Fox, William, *From Bones to Bodies*. H. Z. Walck, Inc., 1959
Mason, George F., *Animal Tools*. William Morrow, 1951
Animal Weapons. William Morrow, 1949
May, Julian, *They Turned to Stone*. Holiday House, 1965
Poling, James, *Animals in Disguise*. W. W. Norton and Co., 1966
Russell, Solveig Paulson, *All Kinds of Legs*. Bobbs-Merrill, 1963
Selsam, Millicent E., *Around the World with Darwin*. Harper and Row, 1960
Storer, John Humphreys, *The Web of Life*. Devin-Adair Co., 1953
Ubell, Earl, *The World of the Living*. Atheneum Pubs., 1965
Zim, H. S., *How Things Grow*. William Morrow, 1960

Acknowledgments

The editors are indebted to the staff of the LIFE Nature Library edition of *Evolution*, from which this volume has been adapted. The staff for this edition was Ogden Tanner, editor; Eric Gluckman, designer; Kelly Tasker and Jonathan Kastner, writers; Eleanor Feltser, Susan Marcus and Theo Pascal, researchers; Grace Fitzgerald, David L. Harrison, copyreaders; Gloria Cernosia du Bouchet, art assistant.